THE 2ND AMERICAN REVOLUTION

Honoring *the* Sacrifices *of* our Founders

William Shuttleworth
CFP, CLU, ChFC, CIC

Pro-Publishing

Imprint of Morgan James Publishing

The 2nd American Revolution
Honoring the Sacrifices of our Founders

ISBN 978-0-98237-932-5

Library of Congress Control Number: 2009936848

Pro-Publishing

Imprint of Morgan James Publishing
1225 Franklin Ave., STE 325
Garden City, NY 11530-1693
Toll Free 800-485-4943
www.MorganJamesPublishing.com

For additional copies of this book, simply email the author at: **thebook@us-founders.us**

Multiple copies are available (for gifts or for group study) at a reduced price if all placed on a single order.

In an effort to support local communities, raise awareness and funds, Morgan James Publishing donates one percent of all book sales for the life of each book to Habitat for Humanity. Get involved today, visit **www.HelpHabitatForHumanity.org**.

Foreword

Signing of the Constitution of the Untied States in 1787: Painting by Howard Chandler

The thirty-nine individuals shown above at the signing of the U.S. Constitution in 1787 had risked their lives, their fortunes, and their sacred honor in order to create a great nation. They then entrusted the preservation and protection of that nation to *"We the People."* Being charged with such a huge responsibility requires that from time to time one step back and consider how they are doing in carrying out their responsibilities. The United States of America is the oldest surviving constitutional republic made up of a federation of states to ever have been formed. When you reflect upon the fact that while the United States comprises just 5% of the population and geographic land area of the **entire world** yet it has created more new wealth than all the rest of the world ***combined,*** one is forced to admit that our founding fathers were on to something when they created this nation!

It is essential that *"We the People"* of the United States ask ourselves, "are we being true to those people who <u>*sacrificed all*</u> to give birth to this great democratic experiment?" In the pages of this book you will be shocked to learn that not only have we failed to preserve and protect the nation that has been entrusted to us, but that *"We the People"* have actually allowed it to be substantially changed from the intent of our founding fathers. We have allowed our nation, and therefore the principles of our founders, to be abused and corrupted; and this abuse and corruption has, most recently, been accelerating out of control.

This past year has been especially difficult for America. America is on hard times, but not for the reason that might first come to mind. Yes, our nation has been experiencing some challenges in the stock, bond, and real estate markets due to the fact that we are currently digesting some past financial excesses. But we have gone through these experiences many times in our history. What most people don't understand is that America's real challenges of today are <u>*not*</u> financial. America's <u>*real*</u> current challenge is that its very survival is at risk.

Please understand and be aware that America is changing and changing very quickly. No one should necessarily be an alarmist, yet we should <u>*all*</u> be realists. We need to examine very closely what is currently transpiring in our government. *"We the People"* have a solemn duty under our Constitution to watch over those with whom we entrust our nation. This book is about America. This book is about our responsibilities as citizens to preserve, protect and defend America from enemies both foreign and domestic. This book is written with a few simple goals in mind. Those goals are to inspire, educate, and motivate the reader to **thought** and to **action**. America remains the same nation today as at her founding: *"The last best hope for man on earth"*. We dare not take this for granted yet I fear that far too many of us have done just that. Read this book. Consider where you believe America stands today relative to when she was founded. Consider where America is headed. Consider carefully whether <u>**you**</u> should become more involved. It is important to constantly bear in mind what one of our nation's founders and her second President, John Adams, told us at the time of our nation's founding: *"A Constitution of Government once changed from Freedom, can never be restored. Liberty, once lost, is lost forever."*

Preface

On July 4, 1776, British subjects in the American colonies made it official. On that day, their representatives signed the Declaration of Independence. These Americans made a courageous yet thoughtful and calculated decision to strike out on their own. The colonists chose to no longer be tethered to a government that they deemed to be ruled by tyrants in a faraway place and whom they determined had lost touch with their needs and their way of life. It was guaranteed to be a high-risk journey fraught with many uncertainties and huge dangers, and to be a journey that would very likely result in certain death to many of them. If all of that weren't bad enough, a great majority of the American colonists felt that the gamble they were about to undertake had very little chance of being successful. Yet despite what appeared to be insurmountable odds, these American colonists, fortified by the courage of their convictions and under the leadership of very brave people, decided the risks were worth taking. These Americans had reached a point at which their patience was totally exhausted. They had given up any hope of positive change, and the circumstances of their current day-to-day life under the rule of the British Crown had become intolerable to them. Worse yet, they saw no relief in sight. In their minds, they were being smothered by a government in a faraway place that was operated by people who were making decisions that they deemed counter to what was in their best interests. The British government was constantly imposing taxes and fees on the American colonists to pay for programs that the colonists believed were of absolutely no benefit to them. The colonists also knew that if they didn't act, and act boldly, their children and grandchildren would meet the same intolerable fate. The very thought that *all future* generations would suffer the same burdens of paying for government programs that were against their principles and way of life was more than the American colonists could bear. They felt they had no choice but to act. Is any of this beginning to sound familiar to *you*? Does any of the above resonate with you given what has been transpiring in America today?

Deep down, these American people of the eighteenth century knew there had to be a better way to live, a better way to be governed. Their discomfort led them to strike out on what was to become the 1st American Revolution. With nothing more than the strength of their convictions, they pledged to each other their lives, their fortunes, and their sacred honor, and they struck out on a very long and very uncertain fight for their Freedom and Independence.

This fight would last some eight long years (1775 to 1783). Just as many of the American colonists had feared, their struggle at various points along the way came very close to meeting with failure and defeat. Yet despite the extreme long-shot odds against them, they prevailed. These brave souls won their Freedom. They had defeated the greatest military power on the face of the earth with seemingly nothing more than their own sheer force of will and their own desire for Freedom, Liberty, and a better life. Their success was nothing short of a miracle.

History Repeats Itself

Fast-forward nearly two and a half centuries and you will now see the patience of these "same" American people once again being frustrated to the breaking point by a government that many Americans consider to be in a faraway place. Washington, D.C., may not be in a faraway place "geographically"; however, it is **very** "far away" as it relates to where the hearts and minds of a great majority of the American people rest today. The American government of the twenty-first century has very clearly lost touch with the needs, desires, hopes, and aspirations of the American people. The American government of today is passing laws and imposing taxes on its citizens to pay for a constant new wave of government spending for programs that many of these Americans consider to be foolish boondoggles. It is a government that in just a recent six-month period alone spent not millions, not billions, but quite literally **trillions** of dollars on programs and policies that these current Americans not only feel go against what is in their best interests, but that are in many cases actually at direct variance with and counter to the Constitution that their brave forefathers laid down their lives for more than two centuries earlier. These same American people in this new twenty-first century are really no different from their forefathers of the late eighteenth century. Just like their forefathers before them, they know that there most certainly must be a better way to live, a better way to be governed. Just as was the case more than two centuries before, there are once again protests in the streets. Tea parties are being held around the nation in this new century that are eerily similar to and in fact are specifically meant to represent those held by the American colonists in Boston, MA just prior to the 1st American Revolution. Yes, just as in the 1770s, there are rumblings afoot of what could be and, in the view of your author, **should be** the beginnings of a 2nd American Revolution. If all goes well, this 2nd American Revolution will be fought and won on a single day without firing a shot. That day is November 2, 2010, the day on which the next United States mid-term congressional elections are held. Remarkably, this 2nd American Revolution can be easily won. The outcome hinges entirely upon the actions of *today's* American citizens. Details will follow in the pages of this book.

Just what constitutes grounds for revolution by the people against their government? Thomas Jefferson, in the second paragraph of the Declaration of Independence, gives us a very **precise** answer. While the other founders made multiple changes to much of Jefferson's original Declaration of Independence, they left this part essentially unchanged from the very words chosen by Jefferson. Thomas Jefferson had this to say on the matter:

> *"Governments are instituted among Men, deriving their just powers from the Consent of the Governed, that whenever any Form of Government become destructive to these Ends, it is the Right of the People to alter or to abolish it, and to institute new Government, laying its Foundation on such Principles, and organizing its Powers in such Form, as to them shall seem most likely to effect their Safety and Happiness. Prudence, indeed, will dictate that Governments long established should not be changed for light and transient Causes; and accordingly all Experience hath shewn, that Mankind are more disposed to suffer, while Evils are sufferable, than to right themselves by abolishing the Forms to which they are accustomed. But when a long Train of Abuses and Usurpations, pursuing invariably the same Object, evinces a Design to reduce them under absolute Despotism, it is their Right, it is their Duty, to throw off such Government, and to provide new Guards for their future security. Such has been the patient sufferance of these Colonies; and such is now the necessity which constrains them to alter their former Systems of Government...."*

So there you have it. Governments are begun by people and get their powers from the **consent** of the governed. If government becomes destructive to the ends for which they were established, **it is the right, it is the duty, of the people** to alter or abolish **that** government and to institute a **new** government. Were Jefferson to have stopped there, one could argue in favor of revolution at most any turn. But he didn't stop there. Jefferson was careful to provide what we shall call a "qualifying statement." He said that experience has proven that men **should suffer** as much evil as they can withstand, over as long a period as possible, and not dissolve government for **"light and transient"** reasons. Jefferson went on to say that, in fact, experience has shown that people are **likely** to suffer for **long periods** rather than to overturn, alter, or abolish their government. **"Patience is a virtue."** After these very careful words of caution, Jefferson clearly stated that *if* the government, after a long series of ***"abuses and usurpations,"*** has designed and pursued the destructive end to the people's life, Liberty, and pursuit of their happiness, that it is ***not just their right, "it is their duty,"*** to overturn, alter, or abolish such government. Your author believes that ***"We the People"*** have arrived at such a place ***in our time*** within the United States of America. In this book, you will find the evidence with which your author intends to prove this claim. Your author does ***not*** call for overturning or abolishing the government of the United States. However, your author ***does call*** for a significant ***altering*** of our government and argues that this is actually the ***only*** means of saving it.

We have been without a real American Revolution since 1776. That is 233 years. Based on the history of most governments, we are long overdue. In many respects, it is something of a miracle that we have survived this long without one. While I would like it to be otherwise, ***"We the People"*** have been suffering a ***"long train of abuses and usurpations"*** by our government, and our leaders are threatening the very future of our great Republic. Our government, most recently in their takeover of much of the banking, insurance, and auto industries, has ignored long-held property rights and ignored the very rule of law. While it appeared for a brief moment that the United States Supreme Court would intervene with some sanity, in the end they themselves rolled over and failed to do the right thing. These actions will most likely dry up credit for the further expansion of our economy. Our government has piled up so much debt on the backs of future generations of Americans that we will have little choice but to default on our empty promises. The Chinese, who hold some ***$3 trillion*** of our debt, laugh in the face of our "promise to pay." ***"We the People"*** must act ***now*** in order to restore any hope of future credibility.

"God forbid we should ever be twenty years without such a rebellion. The people cannot be all, and always, well informed. The part which is wrong will be discontented, in proportion to the importance of the facts they misconceive. If they remain quiet under such misconceptions, it is lethargy, the forerunner of death to the public liberty.... What country before ever existed a century and half without a rebellion? And what country can preserve its liberties if their rulers are not warned from time to time that their people preserve the spirit of resistance? Let them take arms. The remedy is to set them right as to facts, pardon and pacify them. What signify a few lives lost in a century or two? The tree of liberty must be refreshed from time to time with the blood of patriots and tyrants. It is its natural manure."

—**Thomas Jefferson**, in a letter to William Stephens Smith, November 13, 1787 referring to Shays' Rebellion

"I hold it, that a little rebellion, now and then, is a good thing, and as necessary in the political world as storms in the physical."

—**Thomas Jefferson**, in a letter to James Madison, January 30, 1787 referring to Shays' Rebellion

Contents

Endorsements and Praise for
The 2nd American Revolution

To: All Americans who are concerned about our nation's future
Re: *The 2ⁿᵈ American Revolution* by William E. Shuttleworth

*"Finally, a work that truly addresses the **real** issues that confront our nation! **The 2ⁿᵈ American Revolution** by William Shuttleworth is written for the "common man" in an enjoyable and easy-to-read format. This book describes how '**We the People**' have strayed far away from the form of government that our founding fathers originally created for us in 1787. But Shuttleworth does not stop there. He also provides **answers** and **precisely** explains what '**We the People**' must do to return to the fundamental principles of the U.S. Constitution. This is a real '**page-turner**' from the beginning of the book to the rear cover! If you, like me, are an American Patriot and have become frustrated with where our nation is headed, do yourself a favor and read this book."*

—William J. Couch
Retired Indiana School Superintendent and U.S. Government Teacher

Re: *The 2ⁿᵈ American Revolution* by William E. Shuttleworth

*"Town hall meetings with passionate and concerned Americans are eerily reminiscent of the unrest in the 1700s when the founders of our country took bold steps to write a Constitution for the United States of America. **The 2ⁿᵈ American Revolution** makes the case that it is time to revert to the simple basic form of '**We the People**' government that was envisioned by our founders.*

"An easy read with numerous quotes and references from icons of democracy, the author leads the reader through the derailment of our government and then proposes that we take our country back by proposing nine specific goals of the 2ⁿᵈ American Revolution. At the top of the list is a call for the removal of as many of the 535 elected incumbent members of the U.S. Congress as is possible in November of 2010.

*"**The 2ⁿᵈ American Revolution** is a timely and important read that I can easily recommend..."*

—David L. Daugherty
The Daugherty Companies, Inc.

"The 2ND American Revolution is a thought-provoking book which tackles the issues of today's America through the eyes of our Founding Fathers in easy to understand terms. Add this book to your knowledge arsenal. The sleeping giant is awake and ready to take his country back!"

—Katy Abram,
Pennsylvania homemaker of Arlen Specter town hall fame, August, 2009

Dedication

It is customary for authors to dedicate their book to certain people who have in some way inspired or influenced them. This task is easy for the author of *The 2ⁿᵈ American Revolution*. There can be no more fitting dedication for ***this*** book than to dedicate it to each and every one of the founding fathers of the United States. The contributions our founders made for not just America but quite literally the ***entire world*** are beyond our ability to measure or to comprehend. In W. Cleon Skousen's book, *The 5000 Year Leap*, he describes how the civilization of the entire world had advanced 5,000 years in a period of just 200 years and that this advancement was primarily driven by the formation of America under the leadership of our founding fathers. Skousen's book is a great read and one that any serious student of history should own. Our founders created for us a nation that contained an environment of Freedom and Liberty under which capitalism and free enterprise could flourish unencumbered or held back in any way by an overreaching or tyrannical government. The result was a period of growth and prosperity that was literally a worldwide miracle and a phenomenon that had never occurred before and has had no rival since. The goal of your author's research was to study America's unique history in an attempt to earnestly ***understand*** what our founding fathers had in mind when they created our nation and its system of government so that he could then determine whether ***"We the People"*** of ***today's*** America were holding true to the principles that our founders set forth in the very beginning of our journey as a nation. Only in truly understanding ***the founders'*** intent can we really know whether ***we*** are honoring the tremendous sacrifices that they have made ***for us***. Your author fears that we have disappointed our founders, and it is his sincere hope that we can return to the ideals, principles, and beliefs that the founding fathers so nobly valued and held true to and which have advanced the cause of mankind throughout the world over these past two-plus centuries.

Your author desires to also dedicate this book to four specific individuals, each of whom has had a significant impact on my life and who as a consequence in a great many varied and meaningful ways have influenced this work. These men are all from the small town of Warren, Indiana: George K. Huffman, Russell E. Gilmer, J. Ben Good, and Gordon Laymon. I consider all of these gentlemen to be valued mentors in my life and I am deeply indebted to their witness and to the legacies of each of their lives in the service of America. These men were of the caliber that Tom Brokaw described in his book ***The Greatest Generation***. They each served our nation during time of war, came home, went to work, and seldom ever mentioned it again. In the pages that follow, you will read stories that will help you better appreciate why these men are mentioned.

About the Author

William E. Shuttleworth is a farmer and self-employed independent insurance agent from Indiana. Shuttleworth thinks of himself as having lived the American dream. Like so many millions of other Americans, Shuttleworth believes that he has been blessed beyond measure simply by virtue of having the good fortune of being born in the United States of America. He likes to say that he "won *life's* lottery" the day he was born and also likes to add that he "won life's lottery" *again* the day he married his wife Linda. Being raised on a farm near a small town in the American Midwest, in many ways, has uniquely equipped people like the Shuttleworth family with an ability to know and understand what the majority of Americans believe and appreciate about this great nation. There is no "blue blood" flowing through these folks' veins. Born to middle-class parents, both William and Linda went to work as soon as the law would allow them to do so (age thirteen), and neither of them has been out of work since.

Early in life, Shuttleworth earned his living in construction as a carpenter, concrete mason, roofer, painter, and so on. He spent ten years studying at both Indiana and Purdue University *part time,* where he earned his respective associate and bachelor degrees while simultaneously being employed *full time,* first in the construction trades and later in the insurance and real estate industries. Shuttleworth served for more than a decade as a bank director on the board of an independent community bank in Indiana. Shuttleworth and his wife continue to live on the farm, and for thirty years, he has earned his living as a self-employed independent insurance agent. William Shuttleworth is a licensed insurance agent, licensed real estate broker, and a Certified Insurance Counselor (CIC), Chartered Life Underwriter (CLU), Chartered Financial Consultant (ChFC), and Certified Financial Planner (CFP).

William E. Shuttleworth
CFP, CLU, ChFC, CIC

Like millions of other Americans, **William E. Shuttleworth** has been extremely frustrated by what he says has been a hijacking and corrupting of our American system of government as well as our American way of life, mostly by what he describes as arrogant, greedy, corrupt, and misguided elitist career politicians in Washington, D.C.

Introduction

Why this book? Why now? Believe it or not, this is an "accidental" book. It came about in response to requests from others to finish what this farmer from Indiana had started in an email to Glenn Beck[1] in March of 2009. That email was a sort of "rant" that your author wrote Glenn in response to a particular law that the U.S. Congress had just passed. March of 2009 was when the U.S. House of Representatives passed a law that would tax a "*specific class*" of U.S. citizens on their income at a rate of **_90_** percent. Surprisingly, what really brought out the anger that led to the rant was **_not_** the 90 percent tax rate, although that would have been reason enough to be furious. What created more anger in your author than the 90 percent tax rate was the sheer, unbridled arrogance and hypocrisy that our so-called representatives in Congress demonstrated in passing this law. The entire episode centered on certain bonuses that had been paid to employees of an American company, American International Group (AIG). The irony of this whole episode was that the people (the U.S. Congress) who now were determined to take the bonuses away had actually been the very people who had granted the bonuses to this "specific class" of U.S. citizen in the first place! Many have argued that what the U.S. House members did was unconstitutional, for they cite that singling out and taxing a "specific class" of people is prohibited in the U.S. Constitution. Either way, passing this law was perfect proof that these so-called representatives of the people in Congress were either extremely arrogant or stupid, or worse yet, both. As far as your author was concerned, it didn't really matter whether members of Congress were arrogant or simply stupid. What really mattered was that something had to be done, and this farmer from Indiana could no longer in good conscience remain silent. Thus was born the following email rant to Glenn Beck:

Below is an email to Glenn Beck by William E. Shuttleworth concerning the lunacy of the U.S. Congress trying to tax American International Group (AIG) employees at a rate of 90 percent on certain bonuses that the Congress *itself* had granted them just two weeks prior. That was the final straw for this fifty-two-year-old farmer from Indiana.

Dear Glenn, Thank you for being the voice for a great many Americans. I am a farmer from Indiana. I was raised on a farm near a small town in the American Midwest. I spent ten years

---

1   At the time this is being written, Glenn Beck is a very popular radio and television talk show host.

*attending college on a part time basis while simultaneously working full time as a self-employed independent insurance agent and real estate broker. I was a great admirer and a huge supporter of Ronald Reagan. For the past thirty years during my adult life and working years I have continued to be self-employed and live on the farm. To say that I am fed up with our elected officials would be an understatement. Like many Americans, I have actually been frustrated for years watching our elected leaders quite literally "sell our country down the river" while lining their own pockets and at the same time doing all they can to insulate themselves from any sort of accountability for their actions. What infuriates a farmer from Indiana more than the money they waste while recklessly bankrupting our nation is the outright unbridled arrogance they seem to flaunt while doing it. When the financial mortgage crisis began to unfold last September, our elected officials did what **this** farmer and many other people consider to be exactly the **wrong** thing. Instead of allowing the financial excesses to **"naturally wring themselves out"** of our economic system, our so-called elected representatives seized the moment to intervene with an insane fix that will most likely only serve to make matters much worse. Simple logic dictates that you cannot repair damages done from unwise lending practices by attempting to **"paper over"** the problem with excessive government borrowing and spending. This is lunacy, it is un-American, and it **must** come to an end. If we continue this behavior, the very existence of our great Republic is at serious risk. **"We the People"** are flirting with disaster.*

"There is no practice more dangerous than that of borrowing money."
—**George Washington,** July 12, 1797

---

*I was fortunate to serve on the board of a local community bank for many years. If I were to cite the most important fundamental principle that I learned during that experience, it would be that you cannot fix mistakes in borrowing and lending by throwing good money after bad. It's akin to trying to cure an alcoholic with another bottle of Wild Turkey; however, this is precisely the approach that our government has been taking recently in attempting to "bail out" our banking and insurance industries. The behavior of our government over the past six months has put this farmer from Indiana over the edge. Our founders by now have to be literally rolling over in their graves. Glenn, the time has now arrived for a **"2nd American Revolution"**.*

The 2nd American Revolution

What do I mean by a 2nd American Revolution? I mean that we must take our government back from the elitist career politicians who have bankrupted our nation by virtue of allowing themselves to be manipulated, bought, sold, and corrupted by many and varied greedy special interest groups. Quite simply, I mean that we must once again begin **following the Constitution** that our founders so courageously fought and died for and **so wisely** created for us. In very simple terms, I mean that we must **dismantle** much of the current federal government and dramatically reduce its size. Our founders, through the Constitution, called for the federal government's role in Americans' lives to be **almost nonexistent**. Essentially the only roles the federal government was to have in the affairs of the people were to provide for the defense of the nation, issue and coin money, handle foreign affairs, and regulate interstate commerce. In other words the federal government was only to have power over and take care of those **very few** items that the people and the states could not accomplish for themselves. The founders were very adamant about severely limiting the role of our central government. In fact, in our Constitution, the founders actually spoke more about what a central government **was not** allowed to do than they did about what it **was** allowed to do. They intended for the American people to live their lives free of any governmental interference. If there were to be decisions made by government, our founders desired that those decisions be made at the very **lowest level** by **local** and **state** governments. The founders of our nation also clearly understood that decisions affecting the everyday lives of people are best made by the specific people that those decisions will impact, primarily the people's **families** and most certainly **not any** form of government. For the majority of our founding fathers, government was considered really nothing more or less than a necessary evil. Thomas Paine, the man who authored the famous pamphlet **Common Sense**, written in January of 1776, evidences our founding father's intent best in the following statement:

> **"Society in every state is a blessing, but government, even in its best state, is but a necessary evil; in its worst state, an intolerable one."** —**Thomas Paine,** *Common Sense*, 1776

These brilliant men understood that there must be **accountability** for decisions made by elected officials. They also understood that accountability can really only best be provided on a very local, face-to-face level. They wrote our Constitution to accomplish this by specifically limiting national government, leaving the bulk of the power in the States. Isn't it amazing how smart these guys were? Actually, we should not be surprised or amazed by their superior intellect for these were exceptionally *learned men. Even so, given the magnitude of what they were able to accomplish, divine providence was very likely at work **in and through** these people.*

What Must Take Place

*Just what must occur and how will this 2ⁿᵈ American Revolution take place? First and foremost, we must **now** do what Newt Gingrich and others in Congress tried but failed to accomplish in the "Contract with America" in 1994. **"We the People"** must insist on having an amendment to the U.S. Constitution that mandates term limits for our elected federal officials. With 80 percent of the American people in favor of term limits, the debate should not be **whether** we will have them, but rather **what form** they should take. My idea is that the U.S. House should be limited to four terms and that the U.S. Senate should be limited to two terms. This would equate to a maximum of eight years for the House and twelve years for the Senate. We may want to change the House terms to four years. This would allow elected officials more time to get things done and not exhaust the representatives and the electorate with nonstop election cycles. In any event, no one person should be allowed to serve longer than twelve years in a federal office. In addition, elected leaders should not be allowed to run for a **new** office while they are serving in their **current** one. Once an elected leader has served two terms in one office, they should not be allowed to run for any other office; the only exception being if we have a real statesman on our hands and that person desires to compete for the presidency. Term limits will **keep ideas fresh by involving <u>more</u> folks**. We will then enjoy the benefits of a true "representative" government. Oh yes, by the way, since there will no longer be career jobs for elected officials, **"We the People"** will no longer provide special pensions for elected officials, nor special health care benefits, nor private gyms and barber shops, no special treatment of any kind. The only compensation will be a stipend or nominal "living wage," just like we had at our founding and up through Abraham Lincoln's day. Lincoln ran for the U.S. House of Representatives in 1846 and he won a two-year term. At that time there was an understanding that, when elected, you served one term and went home and back to work in the "real world." Despite the fact that Lincoln **loved** the job and would probably have been reelected, he honored the tradition and did not seek a second term. We need to return to those days of the **"citizen"** statesman. In our new and improved system, we will once again have elected officials who are not in it for the money and power but rather to simply serve their country. And let's face it, once we get finished dismantling much of the federal government, there will not be that much for these people to do. Oh yes, one other thing, elected officials will now govern from their **home districts**. With today's modern computer technology, meetings can be held via teleconference literally from the official's "home office." All of* *their telephone calls and teleconferences will be held on an "open line." That way, any American can dial in and "listen in" **at will**. This will result in total transparency and will make it easier for our public servants to avoid corruption. Washington, D.C., will pretty much become a "museum" where the president lives and where Congress meets a few times each year.*

*Second, we **must** dismantle much of the U.S. federal government. While this dismantling will take some time to complete, the final result will be more than worth the effort. Within a short time, over half of what the federal government now "**attempts**" to do for the people will be done much more **efficiently and effectively** on a local level by families, churches, and neighborhoods or by local and state governments. The result will be that we will once again have the Federalism that our founders gave us originally and that Ronald Reagan so wisely reminded us that we needed to restore. Social Security will "over time" gradually be privatized. Federal programs such as Medicare, Medicaid, welfare, unemployment (and the list goes on and on ad infinitum) will **cease to exist** on a federal level. Family, friends, neighbors, churches, and local governments will provide these services for people on an entirely **local** level where **accountability** will once again be possible. There are many details to be worked out, but you get the idea. We are going to revert back to the system that our founders created for us originally and that they outlined so eloquently for us in our United States Constitution. This system worked exceedingly well for us during the course of more than the first half of our existence as a nation, and there is no reason to believe that it won't work again. Critics will say that this approach won't work, that this is a "different time." They will argue that the American people of today won't care for their own, that they won't pick up where the government leaves off. They will say that society will break down, that anarchy will result. I completely and totally reject this premise. To the contrary, I have a deep and abiding faith in the American people. If **"We the People"** simply get the federal government out of the way of the people, we will unleash **the miracle that is America**. The ideals and principles that our founders used in creating our great nation are **unchanging** and **timeless**. These same ideals and principles will work just as well in **our** current time as they did more than two centuries ago during **their** time.*

Third, we must honor our obligations. That begs the following question: What are we going to do about the now more than $12 trillion of debt that our politicians have created while corrupting our system and wasting our money? That's real simple, we will pay it off. There's a new and novel idea for you. Something dawned on me while I was driving down the California coast one day this past winter. As I drove for miles and miles along the Pacific Ocean enjoying the sunset, I couldn't help but notice that there was nothing anywhere to be seen. By this I mean there were no buildings, no roads, *no people, nothing. This was not particularly unusual because I was driving through a military base. The federal government owns some of the most **desirable** and **valuable** real estate in the United States; and they own **LOTS** of it! Whatever **"We the People"** are doing on this **prime** real estate (with the exception of Navy bases) can just as easily be accomplished on some of the **ugliest** real estate in the United States, which the federal government also owns—areas like the Arizona and Nevada deserts. So no problem; we will simply move these functions to the less desirable **ugly** real estate and sell off the extremely valuable **prime** real estate to private developers and use those funds to help pay off the national debt. Keep in mind that selling valuable, prime real estate is just <u>one</u> idea. Once the process begins, **"We the People"** will be able to come up with **endless** lists of excellent ways to save money, raise funds, sell off government assets, completely eliminate government programs, etc. It will actually be a very enjoyable and liberating experience dismantling the federal government. This process will be much like private sector bankruptcy reorganization, only on a national scale. If there's money left over when we are finished, we can create a federal surplus to be used for future defense needs or we can hand the excess money over to the states on a per capita basis to pay for the unfunded Social Security and Medicare liabilities that they are going to have to figure out how to cover. While we are at it, we will also by now have put in place a federal balanced budget amendment and a presidential line item veto for the budget process to protect ourselves from ever again having to suffer from this sort of insanity in our future.*

*You may have noticed that I have been picking on the Congress. Not to worry, similar restrictions will be placed on the presidency. The presidency will take on a much more conservative and modest air. Just as in the case of the Congress, much of what the president has been occupied with will no longer be required. Since most of what **both** branches have been doing will be returned to the states, eliminated, or privatized, much of our bloated federal bureaucracy will likewise no longer be necessary and will cease to exist. Just think, no longer will the president spend a cool million dollars of taxpayer money flying Air Force One back and forth to Denver or Phoenix simply to celebrate spending $787 billion on a stupid and needless stimulus package full of pork projects that shouldn't have been passed in the first place! In this new environment of **back to basics** government, such folly will not even cross the president's mind. Won't that be great?*

Fourth, we must revert back to the days when we actually followed the U.S. Constitution. We owe this not just to the rule of law but also to the honor and the sacrifices of our founders. The founders of our Republic were willing to make enormous personal sacrifices in creating this nation of ours. We have disrespected them tremendously by our actions. What is equally important is that our actions *also dishonor the sacrifice made by the generations who have come before us, our forefathers, who died on the battlefield and who gave of themselves so selflessly. This current insane behavior by our federal government is unsustainable and will come to an end very soon **one way or another**. Our founders wisely warned us that if the American people were not vigilant, the consequences that **"We the People"** are **now experiencing** would at some point occur in our future. We should not be surprised these brilliant men would be correct in their predictions. Many will say that this dream of a 2ⁿᵈ American Revolution occurring on a peaceful basis, as outlined above, is simply a pipe dream. Perhaps they are correct. Only time will tell. There is one thing that **is** certain. The course we are now on will **most certainly** result in **some form** of a 2ⁿᵈ American Revolution. Let us hope and pray that we can shepherd our great nation through it peacefully and with honor.*

William E. Shuttleworth, Warren, IN

I didn't really expect that Glenn Beck would respond to this email, and Glenn didn't disappoint me. However, at the same moment I sent the email to Glenn, I also simultaneously sent it to several friends and acquaintances. The email struck a nerve with many of these folks. They forwarded it to several additional people. Before long I was hearing from people all over America who had read the email and wanted to hear more. You see, these people, along with literally millions of other hard-working Americans, were also **fed up** with what had been transpiring. Many of these folks were now encouraging me to write more on the subject and to make a project of the issue. It led to a great deal of research, and that is how this "accidental book" was born.

I have never authored a book, and I had no earthly idea that there was a book "in me." However, I did have a sincere desire to do what I could to help save our great nation and was thereby motivated to make the effort. All that was left to do was to write the book. Less than a year later, the book was born. A "ghost writer" did not write this book. Your author wrote every word of it, except the most important and powerful words, those being the words of our founders. **They** are the **"real"** authors. Absent the founder's words, the effort would not have been necessary. It was for them that this work was undertaken. I hope that you enjoy the book. More importantly, I sincerely hope that you will embark on this journey with me to **save** our Republic.

Before you begin reading Chapter 1, your author recommends that you go to Chapter 10 at the end of this book and read **"A Nine (9) Point Plan to Save America from an otherwise**

Certain Demise, *"* as this is the *"**heart and soul**"* of <u>***The 2nd American Revolution***</u>. Reviewing these nine (9) goals ***first*** will provide you an excellent "primer" and outline. This information will most certainly be of help to you in better understanding the intent and thesis of the ***entire*** book. You will find included in this book, in their original form and spelling, the Declaration of Independence and the Constitution of the United States. These documents are there for your active review and reference. The strength of these documents lies in their brevity. These documents form the entire basis for our nation's existence; yet combined they are just seventeen standard pages in length. Both documents ***combined*** are seventeen pages in length, as compared to the $787 billion economic stimulus bill of March 2009 at over 1,000 pages or the IRS income tax code, which comprises more than 66,000 pages. We all have much to learn from our founders in many areas. Perhaps we should start with their lesson of being succinct. These documents have been placed at the very ***"center"*** of the book, between Chapters 5 and 6, rather than at the end of the book, as is often customary. Their placement in the center of the book is by design, to remind us that ***"We the People"*** need to keep these documents *"**at the very center**"* of all we say and do as we go about conducting the business of our great nation. Let us now begin with Chapter 1.

Chapter One
Setting Some Ground Rules for this Book

It is important that we clear the air about something from the outset. This is not meant to be a "political" book. By that, I mean these writings are not intended to promote one political party or political philosophy over any other. Your author has no "axe to grind" with *any* political figure or *any* political party. This book is simply about what is best for *America*. In the interest of full disclosure, and as you read in the email to Glenn Beck that appeared in the introduction, your author was a great admirer and an unapologetic supporter of Ronald Reagan. From that, you might have concluded that I consider myself to be a member of the Republican Party. You may have further concluded that this would be a book with a goal of convincing you to embrace the philosophy of the Republican Party. If those were your conclusions or assumptions, you have been wrong. Please understand; during the Reagan era, I did indeed consider myself to be a Republican. Now, however, I feel as though I am a man *without* a party. Ronald Reagan pointed out in his explanation of why he had changed from a Democrat to a Republican that he hadn't left the Democratic Party, it had left him. I have that same sensation today. I have not left the Republican Party; the Republican Party has left me. I am therefore currently a man without a party.

As I see it, when measured against what our founders had in mind for us, there is *not one whit* of difference between the two major political parties in this country. They have *both* lost their way. For my purposes, they may as well consider themselves as one party under the name of either the "*Dempublicans*" or "*Republicrats.*" While I am especially shocked as well as fed up with the actions taken by Barack Obama since he became president, you should also know that I have been equally or perhaps even more angry with the actions taken by George W. Bush and the Republicans. We could have expected what we have gotten from Barack Obama. But George W. Bush was disingenuous. George W. Bush and the Republicans claimed to be conservative, yet they governed as socialists. George W. Bush's presidency was, as this farmer from Indiana sees it, *a very big lost opportunity*. George W. Bush governed at a time when he could have made a real difference for this nation but he failed to "seize the moment." He could have vetoed spending, but he didn't. He could have taken steps to protect our borders and stop illegal immigration, but he didn't. He could have focused on the ***real war on terror*** by exclusively hunting down and killing Osama bin Laden and Al-Qaeda, but he didn't. He could have let the mortgage crisis run its ***natural*** course, but he didn't. George Bush did keep us safe after 9/11 and for that we can all be grateful and thankful. But make no mistake; I am just as disappointed and angered with George W. Bush and the Republicans' behavior as I am with the behavior of Barack Obama and our other so-called representatives in Congress. We have ***big*** problems to solve. These are ***not*** the people to solve them.

"US-Founder's" Party

For all of the reasons stated above, I now consider myself to be a member of the "US-Founder's" Party. You are probably saying, ***"I have never heard of the US-Founder's Party."*** That's because it doesn't exist. Do you realize that there are more than a hundred political parties in the United States? It seems that there is a political party for every splinter group you can put a name to. Unfortunately, there is not one political party, with the possible exception of the Constitution Party, which ***truly*** focuses on and makes every effort to follow the U.S. Constitution and the principles, tenets, and beliefs of our nation's founders—that is, until now. With more than a hundred political parties already in existence in the United States, you might be asking, why create one more? We need to create a new one for the simple reason that none of our current political parties stand for redeeming our great nation from the error of our past and present ways. I see it as the only way to right our wrongs. ***We must be bold***. We have evolved to where we are today, slowly and incrementally, over a period of mostly the past seventy to eighty years. However, the only way for us to bring our nation back to the roots of our founders will be to make some very ***dramatic and bold*** moves. There are simply too many firmly entrenched special interest groups in place for us to accomplish it in any other manner. Besides, the people currently in power in the Democrat and Republican parties will not give up easily. Our elitist career politicians firmly believe they are just the people needed to solve our nation's problems. These people think that even larger government and, more specifically, the new government programs that ***they*** create are just the prescription that will cure our nation's ills. There are also millions of well-meaning people who steadfastly believe, despite all of the clear and consistent overwhelming past evidence proving they are dead wrong, that ***more and bigger*** government is the answer. The actions of our elected leaders have been insane; for as we all know, insanity is doing the same thing over and over again and expecting a different result. Our current elected officials and their contemporaries will not go away quietly. What this country needs is a grass-roots movement under strong *new* leadership with a very bold *new* agenda of major reforms in government, beginning with the passage of a Term Limits Amendment to the Constitution for our elected and appointed federal officials, significant reductions in government programs and spending, a Balanced Budget, and a Presidential Line Item Veto Amendment, as well as many other reforms that you will read about in this book. This 2ⁿᵈ American Revolution will not be about ***"tinkering at the margins or nibbling at the edges"*** of our national problems. Our past few decades of mismanagement require that we make <u>***wholesale***</u> changes in how our government operates and functions. It is simply not realistic to expect that any of our current incumbent politicians have the ***wisdom*** or the ***courage*** to make good decisions for our nation going forward. They have been entirely derelict in their duties, and their services are therefore no longer needed. What the United States now needs is a new approach to governance under the leadership of a new set of common sense: "***citizen***" statesmen. We need people who are motivated solely by what is in the best interest of the future of our great nation. There is only one means of fighting a successful revolution, and that is with revolutionaries. Fighting a revolution requires not caretakers, but people who ***really care***. Now all of that being said, and to be totally fair, I would not rule out the possibility that our two major political parties might put forward candidates who are real reformers. Governors Rick Perry of Texas and Sarah Palin of Alaska would be included in a list of possible people. But take note that these folks come from the states, not the federal government. I have serious doubts about the two parties' ability to fill the roles needed from their current ranks and most particularly those already in office. The big money and special interests are simply too well entrenched within these establishments to allow the two major parties to stray very far away from the status quo—and don't forget, it's the status quo that is <u>***killing***</u> America. This revolution, like every successful revolution, will require true revolutionaries to fight and to win it. That is why I am suggesting that we need a new political party. What more fitting name could it have than the **"US-Founder's Party"**?

I mentioned earlier that I consider myself to be a man without a party. In a great many ways, I feel as though I am a man without a country and actually often think of myself as a man living in a foreign land. Hearing me say that I feel like a man without a country or living in a foreign land may sound extreme to you. I hope that it does. It is intended as such. While I in no way feel that I have left America, in a great many ways, I feel that America has left me. Neither of the two major political parties truly supports the fundamental principles of our nation's founders, yet they are running our nation. It is for this reason that I say in many respects I consider myself to be a man living in a foreign land. Our elected leaders have slowly and insidiously moved away from following our Constitution. As a result, America is not the same country that I grew up in and learned to love and appreciate so much as a child and young adult. It deeply saddens me and literally breaks my heart to witness that *"We the People"* have allowed America to drift so far away from the principles that in our early beginnings made us the greatest nation on the face of the earth. I am totally confident that if Ronald Reagan were living today, he would share these same sentiments. I know that millions of Americans are also deeply concerned about these matters.

"A little matter will move a party, but it must be something great that moves a nation."
—**Thomas Paine,** *Rights of Man,* 1792
Born in England in 1737—Died in America in 1809

"The cause of America is, in a great measure, the cause of all mankind."
—**Thomas Paine,** *Common Sense,* 1776

What You Can Expect from This Book

There has been much said lately by many different individuals and groups on the subject of the government's activist intervention in our economy and in the individual daily lives of our people. There has been no shortage of yelling, screaming, complaining, and gnashing of teeth by politicians and the talking heads on television about what the government has been doing or not doing. However, what has been *so glaringly absent* from all of this noise have been any meaningful, specific, concrete ideas, or suggestions on what *should* have been done in contrast to what *has* or *has not* been done. As a result, in the view of your author, *all* of these people have been quite simply wasting their time. These people have only been *"tinkering at the margins and nibbling at the edges"* of the real central problems that confront our nation. What you will find in this book are the author's observations of where we have gone wrong as a nation, but only as filtered through the eyes of our founding fathers.

More importantly, however, you will also find at the end of each chapter specific suggestions and specific recommendations on solutions designed to *fix* the many problems that confront

America. Please understand that I am under no illusion that you will agree with everything that I have to say; however, I can guarantee that you will enjoy "the read." Many of the comments, suggestions, and ideas in this book you will very likely *not* have heard before now. Many of the solutions that will be offered in this book you might believe to be unconventional or even impractical. That is okay. The problems that we face in our nation are *enormous,* and they will require *bold measures* as well as thinking and approaches to problem solving that are "outside the box" of conventional reasoning. My primary goal in writing this book is to simply get people to *think* and *act.* When you are finished reading this book, you will clearly understand where this farmer from Indiana stands on solving our nation's problems. It is also my sincere desire that you will have a much better appreciation of how awesome and thoughtful our founders and forefathers were. What is being proposed involves some very *fundamental* changes to our current political system as well as to our very system of government. For this reason, much of what is proposed will be viewed by many of you as radical, impossible to achieve, or both.

That said, please bear in mind that __all__ of what is proposed is based upon what our founders and forefathers had to say on the matter. In this book, you will be hearing *directly* from the founders of this great nation, from many of our wise forefathers (like Abraham Lincoln), from many of the other great minds from our nation's past, and from some of our current leaders who are still alive and doing well today. If you are like millions of other Americans, you are very likely extremely frustrated with the direction in which our nation is headed. You realize America is on the wrong track, but you are at a loss as to what to do or how to help bring her back. This book will provide you great *relief.* Don't worry; you will not be required to run for office. All that is required of you in order to play a critical role in bringing America back from the brink of otherwise certain destruction and demise is to go to the polls on November 2, 2010, and *vote.* It is really just that simple! Vote, and you will be a soldier in the silent revolution to take back America. If enough of us exercise our right to vote, on that very day we will begin to release America from her bondage to debt and misery and put her back on track for a *brilliant future.* While reading this book will be a sad and sobering experience due to the truth telling about how we have allowed America to fail her founders and our heritage, the work here is also about the real *possibilities* we have for correcting the error of our ways and rebuilding America back to her former glory. It __can__ be done.

Here Is Just One Example of a Proposed Change

One example of what you will find in this book is a proposal that ***"We the People"*** join together in a grass-roots movement to insist that the U.S. Congress vote on and pass an amendment to the U.S. Constitution limiting the terms of our U.S. House Representatives and Senators. Your author sees this as the ***only way*** to fix our current corrupt political system. My position is that by virtue of allowing politicians to make a career of their positions as elected officials, over time we have really accomplished nothing more than to replace a royal monarchy of the eighteenth century with a new royal oligarchy of the twenty-first century. As a result, most all of our elected officials have lost touch with and are actually totally clueless about what their constituents think, much less what those constituents expect from them. The reality of this is proven every day by what they say and do. Despite this, these elected officials enjoy a 95 percent lock on reelection. This needs to change, and with 80 percent of the nation's population now in favor of term limits, it appears that the time is finally right to bring it to pass.

There was a time when our country was first founded that politicians sought elective office for all of the ***right*** reasons. They ran to serve their country and to truly represent their constituents at home. They limited their terms ***voluntarily***. As a result, we had a healthy democratic Republic due to the fact that ***we had a constant flow of fresh ideas and truly representative government***. Perhaps the best, and likely the most famous, example of this was the case of Abraham Lincoln. Lincoln was elected to the U.S. Congress in 1846 as a U.S. House Representative from Illinois. He absolutely loved the job and would have preferred to run for reelection in 1848. Setting his personal desires aside, Lincoln stood down and allowed others to run and serve in his district. During that time in our history, it was understood that you served your term and then went home and ***"back to work in the real world."*** As a result of this long-held tradition, the United States had a government that was a true representative Republic during the first century and more of her existence.

Unfortunately, during the course of the twentieth century, we have replaced that tradition and have evolved into a career political system with a more than 95 percent reelection rate for incumbents. In the process, we have lost any real semblance of a representative democracy as well as any chance to have a constant flow of fresh ideas ***"bubbling up from the people,"*** as was the case in the early days of our Republic. The result of this has been an insidious brain drain and a "dummying-down" of our government. The only real solution to fix this problem is to simply make it ***illegal*** to stay in office as a career. This can easily be accomplished via an amendment to the U.S. Constitution. In addition, we will no longer provide elected leaders fast-vesting lifetime pensions, private dining rooms, cradle-to-grave health care, personal barber shops, private gyms, big staffs, and a list of special treatments too long to list here. More details will follow in this book.

> *"The happiness of society is the end of government."* —**John Adams,** 1776

> *"Whenever the people are well informed, they can be trusted with their own government; that whenever things get so far wrong as to attract their notice, they may be relied on to set them to rights."* —**Thomas Jefferson** in a letter to Richard Price, January 8, 1789

The United States Constitution

"We the People" have allowed our elected leaders to *abuse* the Constitution. In our early days as a nation, the Constitution was referred to often and the people required that their elected leaders *follow it*. Thomas Jefferson felt that the Tenth Amendment within the Bill of Rights, which limits the powers of the national government and reserves all rights that are not specifically granted to the national government within that document to the states and to the people, formed the *very essence* of the document. We have now allowed it to be interpreted *exactly in the reverse* of this intent. The Tenth Amendment was placed there with the express purpose to avoid what the thirteen American Colonies were forced to endure under British rule. Our founders specifically intended that any political decisions be made at the very *lowest level* in society, where *accountability* is possible and government control could be maintained. Our Constitution, if it is anything, is a document of negatives *limiting* the national government. This fact has frustrated aggressive political leaders since our founding, and it continues to be a great source of frustration to them today. That was *precisely the intent* of our founding fathers. It wasn't as though they were trying to be sadistic; they simply valued Freedom and Liberty above all else, and they had the wisdom to know what would happen if these rules were not adhered to. Should not *"We the People"* honor their wishes? By the way, the General Welfare clause said *"promote"* the General Welfare, <u>*not*</u> *"provide"* the General Welfare.

Ballots, not Bullets

Our founding fathers during the 1st American Revolution were left with but *one* choice. Their fight for Freedom, Liberty, and the change that they desired would of necessity have to be fought and won with bullets, as well as the shedding of their own blood. Fortunately, *"We the People"* of America in the twenty-first century have the luxury of an entirely *different* course of action. *We* are able to redeem our Freedom and Liberty and bring about the change that *"We the People"* desire simply by *becoming more engaged* and casting ballots in a box. Ours will be that of a _silent_ revolution. *"We the People"* will simply show up in enormous and unprecedented numbers, and vote. Once again, the American people will revolutionize the world. *"We the People"* of the twenty-first century are in this enviable position because of the sacrifices of our founders in the 1st American Revolution *and* due to their forming our entirely unique system of government under the U.S. Constitution. It is the sincere hope and prayer of this farmer from Indiana that our 2nd American Revolution will be fought and won, not with the shedding of blood, but rather with an active and engaged electorate who are dedicated to honoring the sacrifices made by those who have come before us. This time around, we can, and we must, use ballots instead of bullets.

"We the People"

Quite frequently throughout this book, you will see the words *"We the People"* shown in this identical format. This has been done purposely and to provide emphasis. It seems that a great many American citizens living today have forgotten, or perhaps never really fully understood, that our system of government was designed so that the *ultimate power* in the decision making for our great nation rests with *"We the People."* This ignorance on the part of many Americans has not necessarily been the fault "of the people." Instead, it has been due to our "collective" neglect in teaching these principles to our citizens through good education. It seems that *"We the People"* no longer insist that our youth are taught the fundamentals of how our system of government operates. However, regardless of where our failures rest, we **_all_** must remember that *"We the People"* are responsible for educating Americans about the HUGE importance of these principles. George Washington reminded us *all* of the *people's power* at our founding in 1787 when he said after the Constitutional Convention:

"The power under the Constitution will always be with the people. It is entrusted for certain defined purposes, and for a certain limited period, to representatives of their own choosing; and whenever it is executed contrary to their interest, or not agreeable to their wishes, their servants can, and undoubtedly will, be recalled."

It was no mistake that our founders began the U.S. Constitution with: *"'We the People' of the United States, in order to form a more perfect union..."* They desired to remind us of **our** power. ***"We the People"*** is being used throughout this book so that we may **all** learn to better appreciate and be constantly reminded of the glorious gift that our founders have given us. In this way, we may each better appreciate the responsibility that we **all** have to honor that gift.

Freedom & Liberty

Throughout this book you will find the words Freedom and Liberty capitalized. Once again, this is done to provide emphasis. One goal of this book is to stimulate a renewed awareness of and appreciation for what our founders and forefathers gave us when they fought and died for our Freedom and Liberty. Therefore, it only seems fitting and proper that we show these words in capital form when these two principles are referred to within the pages of this book. Besides, at the time of our founding, nouns were very often capitalized when they appeared in written form. You will see the evidence of this later as you read the U.S. Constitution that appears in the center of this book in its original form. I have also included the Declaration of Independence in the same section of this book.

Chapter Two
How America Has Lost Her Way

What Went Wrong?

Just after the Revolutionary War, and continuing for more than a century thereafter, *"We the People"* held true to what our founders had given us. What our founders so thoughtfully provided us was a *"true representative Republic."* Then, early in the twentieth century, we began to allow our Freedoms to be taken away, and our nation slowly but surely migrated toward a *socialist* state in which we forfeited our rights to control our own individual destiny. Perhaps we did this unwittingly; however, either way, we slowly and surely gave up what Abraham Lincoln so eloquently described as a nation *"of the people, by the people, and for the people."* One issue at a time and one election at a time, we gradually *allowed* our government to be transformed from a representative Republic to a royal oligarchy governed by a set of elitist career politicians with a mentality that they know better than the citizen as to what is in that citizen's best interest. We have become *a lazy and apathetic people* who have gradually, yet willingly, surrendered the greatest gift that God has ever bestowed upon a people—that gift being the Freedom to live our lives unmolested by a tyrannical government. The time is <u>**now**</u> for each of us to wake up and to once again become active in determining the destiny of our great nation. *"We the People" must* become engaged. It is time for "Mr. Smith" to go to Washington, for many of us to become *"citizen"* statesmen.

How have *"We the People"* gotten ourselves into this mess? What is keeping us from waking up and doing the right thing? Why are we not willing to become engaged and to force the changes that deep down we know are much needed? Why have we become lazy and apathetic? Will we wait to take action until after it is *too late?* At what point will it have become too late? Where will we find national leaders who have the courage to lead us out of our denial and current bondage to debt? These are all very difficult questions, *yet there are answers*.

What *"We the People"* Need Is a "National Intervention"

Most of us are familiar with the concept of a family intervention, in which an entire family gathers to confront a loved one about that loved one's self-destructive behavior in an effort to save him or her from certain death due to their abuse of drugs or alcohol. Very often, prior to these interventions, there has been a long-running cycle of denial for a very significant period of time on the part of *everyone* in the room. The loved one for years has denied that he or she has a problem. The family members have become "enablers" to the loved one by denying to themselves and to the world around them that the loved one has any sort of problem. That denial must first be **confronted and conquered** by *all* of the parties involved before any *real* progress can begin. Otherwise, the loved one will never be able to take the "next steps" necessary to make any progress toward recovery. Likewise, each of the family members continues to create an environment in which their loved one falls back into dependency because it is "comfortable and familiar" to *them*. This all sounds sick, weird, and twisted; and believe me, *it is*. You must by now be asking, *"What does this story of addiction in a family have to do with what's wrong with America?"*

America's Debt Addiction

The answer to the above question is really quite simple: ___America is addicted to debt___. *"We the People"* of the United States are the family members and our loved one, in this case America, is addicted to debt. And just as in the case of a drug or alcohol addiction, *all* parties are in denial. Nobody wants to be the first to admit that we *all* have a problem. We have *all* become very comfortable living beyond our means. Besides, facing the problem will require that we must ___do something___ to *fix* it. Oh, but you might say that the politicians and the talking heads on television speak about debt all of the time in our constant public debate. Yes, they do; however, they speak of it in a sort of abstract sense with an implied acceptance that the debt really doesn't matter. In fact, our recent vice president, Dick Cheney, made the statement a short while back that *"deficits don't matter."* Well, as much as I hate to be the person to tell everyone, deficits *do* matter. Debt *does* matter. Living beyond your means *does* have consequences. There *will* be a day of reckoning. We saw the reality of this most recently in the case of the mortgage meltdown. We then saw it play out again in the failure of the auto industry. But have you noticed what *really* occurred? What *really* occurred is that *"We the People"* didn't truly face *either* of these problems. Instead, we continued the denial of our addiction by simply adding more debt to *both* of them. When it became obvious that fundamental financial rules had been broken and that we must now face the consequences, *"We the People"* chose to deny the reality of the problem and to once again delay the inevitable. Instead of admitting the real problem and doing the right thing, *"We the People"* chose to postpone facing reality by simply borrowing *more* money. We chose to *transfer* these failures from the *private* sector to the *public* sector by piling mountains of debt onto the backs of *future generations* of the American people. As a result of living in denial, we now have state-run banks, state-run insurance companies, and state-run automobile manufacturing companies. This is all *socialism* and it is *un-American*. Much of it is very likely *unconstitutional*. To put it mildly, our founders would __not__ be pleased. Once again, we have *dishonored* the sacrifices of the founders of our great nation by virtue of our *reckless* and *illegal* actions.

> *"I say, the earth belongs to each of these generations during its course, fully and in its own right. The second generation receives it clear of the debts and incumbrances of the first, the third of the second, and so on. For if the first could charge it with a debt, then the earth would belong to the dead and not to the living generation. Then, no generation can contract debts greater than may be paid during the course of its own existence."*
> —**Thomas Jefferson** in a letter to James Madison, September 6, 1789

"We the People" of the United States are in a national denial and we are in *desperate* need of an intervention. Not one of us should be surprised that so many of our citizens have gotten themselves into serious financial trouble. All that is required to figure this one out is to look at who has been setting the example for our citizens. The leaders of our national government, by their own actions, have *trained* each of us to live beyond our means. In many cases, they have not only taught us by their own example to live beyond our means, they have also actively encouraged us to do so! For example, our national leaders instructed both Fannie Mae and Freddie Mac to make "no-money-down" home loans to a great many people in this country so those people would buy homes that they actually could *not afford* and had *no business* buying in the first place. Our nationally elected leaders in the U.S. Congress, with a more-than-willing accomplice in the president of the United States, have run our nation into a bottomless abyss of debt and into a national bankruptcy. Meanwhile, *"We the People"* have stood by and *allowed* it to happen. We could have stopped it, but we didn't. So ask yourself a question: Would you in your wildest dreams ever have allowed your wife, your husband, your sister, or your brother to go down to the local bank to borrow endless amounts of money *in your name*, thereby forcing

you into personal bankruptcy? If not, why then have *you* allowed your national government to do the exact same thing to you? Driving you into personal bankruptcy is precisely what you have allowed the government to do to you. You have actually done it to yourself, for "*We the People*" *are* the government. Are you prepared to take any action against this in the future, or are you now willing to allow your elected leaders to go forward with bankrupting your children and your children's children? You and I are totally responsible for what has occurred in our nation, and we are likewise totally responsible for bringing it to an end. The buck stops with "*We the People*." "De'Nial" is not just a river in Egypt. Denial is where you and I have been living while we have allowed our national leaders to recklessly drive our country into national bankruptcy. So there is your intervention. There is your reality check.

Is There Any Good News Here? Yes, *"We the People"* <u>Can</u> Fix This

In the opinion of this farmer from Indiana, *"We the People" can* redeem ourselves from the mistakes of our past. We *can* take control of our nation's future and put ourselves back on a strong, solid footing. It won't be easy. Nothing worthwhile is ever easy. However, the payoff will be *more* than worth the effort. The payoff will be that we will have secured the future of our great nation. The payoff will be that we will be honoring the sacrifices of our founders. The payoff will be that we will leave our children and our grandchildren the same birthright that was given us and that we have been so blessed to enjoy during *our* lifetimes. Make no mistake; it is incumbent upon each one of us that we honor the sacrifices of our founders. More important, we *must* leave the gift of our great democratic experiment with the same secure future that it had when we inherited it from those people who came before us. As Thomas Jefferson would say, "*It is our right, <u>it is our duty</u>*." In point of fact, *"We the People"* have a very *solemn obligation* to right these wrongs. *It must* be done and it must be done *very soon*. In this book, you will find the specific action plans necessary to allow us to once again make things right, to redeem our great God-given gifts of Liberty and Freedom and to secure those gifts for future generations of Americans.

It is interesting that at *precisely* the same moment in time that "*We the People*" have finally endured enough of government at every level getting bigger and more repressive of our rights as citizens that the ultimate financial limitations of government's excessive growth through borrowing has also reared its ugly head, *forcing* us to take action. In other words, even if "*We the People*" had not already decided that our experiment with socialism should end, the inherent financial limitations have brought it all crashing down around our ears anyway. Perhaps we needed *both* to occur simultaneously in order for us to face reality and be brought to our senses. Either way, we have arrived at a point in time where we are left with *no choice* other than to face the fact that *we are broke*. Attempting to sustain and further expand socialism in America is now entirely out of the question and is no longer even an option, lest we choose to forfeit our very Republic and, of course, along with it, our way of life. Make no mistake; *"We the People"* *__will__* rise above this crisis. We have overcome graver calamities, such as the Civil War, World War I, and World War II. Repairing this mistake will require great sacrifice, but none more difficult or burdensome than those endured by the brave generations of Americans who have preceded us. Each and every one of those earlier generations have left our beloved American nation better off than when they received it from the prior generation. *We* can, and *we must*, do no different. If we fail to repair this fiscal mess that *we* have created and not *restore* our unique American Freedom and Liberty, ours will be a generation of leaving a legacy of sowing the seeds that will lead to America's demise. That outcome is *totally and utterly* unacceptable. As a citizen, I look forward to the challenge of repairing America. It will be a rewarding and gratifying experience. The process will reawaken the sense that, together, we can overcome anything simply because we are, after all, *__Americans__*. It will require us to once again focus on the fundamental principles that made America the miracle that it was on the day of its founding and that America still remains even in our day, that being: *"The last best hope for man on earth."*

Annual U.S. government spending *doubled* in less than ten years between the years 2000 and 2009. It grew from consuming *33 percent* of the U.S. gross domestic product (GDP; the gross domestic product is the sum total of all the goods and services produced by a nation in any given year) to *__45__ percent* of the U.S. gross domestic product in that same period. During the depression and throughout the entire decade of the 1930s, federal government spending only comprised around 20 percent of gross domestic product. Prior to the 1930s, U.S. government spending was typically *__less than 10 percent__* of gross domestic product. During just the last one third (1/3) of our existence as a nation, *"We the People"* have allowed the federal government to grow by over *400 percent* and consistently consume *45 percent* of the nation's economy! Your elected leaders have led you down this path slowly and very *insidiously* over a period of seventy or eighty years. We now must ask ourselves, at what point will *"We the People"* wake up some morning having completely relinquished *all* of our Freedom and Liberty to government? My friends, we have *already* arrived at that point. There is no reason to *__ever__* *__allow__* federal government spending to exceed 20 percent of our gross domestic product.

If we are to accomplish this, it needs to be the goal of our nation to *immediately* reduce and eliminate U.S. federal government spending, put in place a balanced budget requirement by amending the U.S. Constitution, and put in place an additional requirement that limits federal government spending to 20 percent of U.S. gross domestic product. After all, forty-nine states *already* have a balanced budget *requirement!* The balanced budget requirement and 20 percent of GDP cap must be *mandated by law* for U.S. government spending. The only very rare exception will be during times of war and then only to allow spending to be out of balance or increase beyond 20 percent of GDP for that part of the federal spending that is *directly attributable* to the cost of the war. This is all simply common sense. In the long run, the federal government is subject to the <u>same</u> economic limitations as you and I. There is no escaping these fundamental laws of finance. Do you think for one minute if your author, this farmer from Indiana, had operated his farm on the same basis that your federal officials have operated your government, that he would still own and be living on his farm today? We all know the answer to that question.

Why do we allow the federal government to perpetually break these laws of economics and finance? It is only because *"We the People"* have, up to now, *chosen* to do *nothing* about it. Unfortunately, *"We the People"* no longer have the luxury of being able to further delay or procrastinate on the matter. We have now reached a moment in time that the future of our very Republic is at stake. Complacency is no longer an option. If we do not act, and *act now*, we will all wake up one morning, scratch our heads, and wonder what went wrong. But it will be too late at that point. Your government will be making *all* of your decisions for you, and they will do it because a "national financial emergency" requires it. They will blame it on the economy or on terrorism or on anything other than their own mismanagement of your U.S. government. Your Freedom and Liberty will be forever lost, and you will be left with no one or no circumstance to blame except your *own failure* to exercise your God-given right to vote and to become engaged. So yes, we *can* fix this; however, it requires that *"We the People"* take action, and *very soon*.

Chapter Three
The United States Is In Heap
BIG Financial Trouble

"As a very important source of strength and security, cherish public credit. One method of preserving it is to use it as sparingly as possible"
—**George Washington,** President of the United States
From his Farewell Address, September 17, 1796
Born in 1732, Washington died in 1799

Just since early 2009, the U.S. federal government has taken over and is running much of the banking industry, much of the insurance industry, and much of the auto industry. Politicians in Washington, D.C., now have their sights set on taking over and running the *entire* U.S. health care industry. The United States of America is fast approaching $12 trillion of debt that we admit to owing and upon which we pay interest. In addition to that, depending upon whom you ask, the United States has another $70 to $90 trillion of unfunded Social Security, Medicare, and Medicaid liabilities. This all totals approximately $300,000 for *every man, woman, and child* in the United States, or $1,000,000 for *every household* in the United States. Our future budget forecasts, even under very rosy and very favorable economic growth estimates, are shown to include annual budget deficits of more than *$1 trillion each year* for the next *several years*. Despite all of this, our federal officials are now taking steps to create even larger mountains of debt by blindly marching into a black hole of guaranteeing health care for every American citizen and illegal immigrant. The credit card of the United States has reached its limit. Do yourself a favor. Go to www.usdebtclock.org on the Internet. Be ready for a major shock to your system.

The Party Is Over

America is not ***going*** broke. America is by every reasonable measure actually ***already bankrupt***. All that is left for ***"We the People"*** to do is to administer the reorganization in that bankruptcy. The jig is up for us. We have reached a point in time where our nation is left with no alternative but to begin a massive reorganization of our government. There is simply ***no way*** going forward that the U.S. government can honor the obligations she has to each of her citizens; nor can she keep the promises she has made to her creditors. ***"We the People"*** ***must*** get our financial affairs in order, and ***time is short***. Any further delay in making the changes needed will very likely result in "killing the goose that lays the golden eggs"—our national economy and ultimately our very system of government. If we long continue our past behavior into the future, ***"We the People"*** will choose to administer this bankruptcy reorganization by virtue of either defaulting on our debt obligations or creating hyperinflation through the unlimited printing of money, or by some combination of these two. Neither of these two options should be acceptable to any of us. In our reorganization, we must pledge to ourselves as well as to our creditors that ***"We the People"*** will ***not*** default on our obligations either by avoiding payment or by creating massive inflation. Instead, we must set things right. Just like an individual or business entity, ***"We the People"*** must liquidate our nation's assets, pay our debts, and begin to live within our collective means. While we are in this bankruptcy liquidation and reorganization, we must also simultaneously reorganize our national government to prevent this from ever again occurring in our future. The first step in this process is to pledge to one another that we will ***no longer*** continue to further burden tomorrow's American citizens with our sins of overindulgence today. Second, we must put forward a plan that honors our past and provides a secure legacy for our future. Third, we must get busy about implementing the reorganization plan; and we must do it sooner rather than later.

All Things Are Possible

Despite all of these very sobering facts, if we act quickly and decisively, ***"We the People"*** ***can*** save this nation's financial future. People often forget, or perhaps they just take for granted, that the United States of America has the most prosperous economy on the face of the earth. A resilient capitalistic free enterprise system is difficult to negatively affect. In fact, despite our constant and repeated past abuses of it, the economy of the United States has ***always*** managed to rebound and come back even stronger and more dynamic than ever. It will take more than a few mistakes in mortgage lending to put the American economy on its knees. Besides, the real threat to America is ***not*** the recent financial crisis. The ***real*** threat or enemy to America is an out-of-control federal government that has been taken over by elitist career politicians who are at heart, socialists. This current crisis, while severe, should be viewed as our final wake-up call to take the much-needed action in our government that is long overdue.

> *"I wish it were possible to obtain a single amendment to our Constitution. I would be willing to depend on that alone for the reduction of the administration of our government to the genuine principles of its Constitution; I mean an additional article, taking from the federal government the power of borrowing."*
> —**Thomas Jefferson** in a letter to John Taylor
> November 26, 1798

On Bailouts and So-Called Economic Stimulus

In September of 2008, the U.S. stock market began to get wobbly and fluctuate wildly. By the end of September, word came out that certain financial institutions in the United States had become insolvent. President George W. Bush and Secretary of the Treasury Henry Paulson announced that they would be recommending to the Congress that **"We the People"** spend $700 billion on a bailout of certain U.S. financial institutions by virtue of buying what they described as "toxic assets" that were held by these financial institutions. Congress called the bailout "TARP" for "Troubled Asset Recovery Program." Actually, this name made perfect sense to farmers from Indiana, for we have always known that one uses a tarp to "***cover things up.***" After first being voted down due to a loud clamor of protests from **"We the People,"** Congress voted a second time and ultimately passed the bill. As it turned out, that was **only the beginning**. That event set the tone and paved the way for the passing of many more spending bills in the Congress over the next few months under both Presidents Bush and Obama, which culminated in a massive $787 billion economic stimulus bill that was rammed through the Congress with not so much as a cursory review by any of the lawmakers. Added together, the U.S. government would spend not just billions, but literally ***trillions*** of dollars on bailouts and "stimulus" plans. This spending might have been all well and good, except for the small detail that **"We the People" didn't have** the trillions to spend. The money would <u>**all**</u> have to be borrowed, resulting in our mortgaging the future of this once great creditor nation to an extent that it will very likely lead to the financial demise of the United States if strong action is not taken and taken ***very soon***.

> **"Were we directed from Washington when to sow and when to reap, we should soon want bread." —Thomas Jefferson,** date unknown

Three Reasons Why *"We the People"* Should <u>Not</u> Be Doing What We Are Doing

1. **We very simply cannot afford what we are doing.** We are out of money. In fact, we were dead broke before all of this current insane spending began. What we are now doing is committing generational theft on our children, grandchildren, and great-grandchildren. *We* are choosing to live large and well beyond our means by borrowing money that *they* will have to repay. Make no mistake; they *will* repay this debt. It is unavoidable. Actions have consequences. Future generations will repay this money through austerity and a much lower standard of living; and they will very likely experience hyperinflation and the destruction of the U.S. currency in the process. Inflation is nothing more than a tax; an *insidious*, but nonetheless very *real,* tax. The higher the inflation rate, the higher the tax. The United States was already in *very BIG* financial trouble well before the most recent round of idiotic spending began. Before the current so-called financial crisis, the U.S. had amassed $10 trillion of debt. On top of that, depending upon who you ask, the U.S. has another $70 to $90 trillion in unfunded Social Security, Medicare, and Medicaid liabilities. We as a nation have made financial promises that we have *no possible way* of keeping. What we have done as a nation is very much like what the automobile companies *attempted* but failed to do, and that ultimately bankrupted them. The only real difference between General Motors and the U.S. government's unfunded financial promises is the sheer size of the fraud. The U.S. government's Ponzi scheme makes General Motors' look like petty theft. No wonder our government thinks it is okay to bail out General Motors. In the sick and twisted logic of an elitist career politician, this somehow justifies his or her own idiotic actions. For all of the reasons stated above, every American citizen should be fighting against this current insane spending with every ounce of their strength for the simple reason that we don't have the money and we cannot afford it . If that is not reason enough, then every American citizen should be fighting against this current insane spending with every ounce of their strength because they believe it to be morally wrong to *steal* from their children, their grandchildren, and great-grandchildren. It is morally wrong and it also dishonors the sacrifices made by our founders when they created this great nation of ours and entrusted it to us.

2. **What we are doing will not work.** If the fact that we cannot afford it weren't reason enough to stop this insane spending, then fight against it for the simple reason that *it won't work*. We are spending all of this money in effort to "paper over" bad decisions made by a whole bunch of misguided, dishonest, or stupid people, many of whom are elitist career politicians and government bureaucrats. What we *should be* doing instead is to simply let these excesses "wring themselves out" of our economy. The pain would be severe but quick and would mostly affect only those who deserve to be affected. Instead, our current approach will mostly affect the innocent—the U.S. taxpayer and future generations of Americans. If the government wanted to do something to help the situation, they should have done the precise *opposite* of what they did. That is, they should have gotten out of the way, *reduced* government spending, and *cut* taxes. <u>*That*</u> would have stimulated the economy. When the stack of cards began to fall in September of 2008, my brother and I were on vacation overseas with our wives. We were watching all of this unfold at home in the U.S. on television from Europe. I will never forget my brother rhetorically asking, "Why is the government spending $700 billion on this? Won't someone in the private sector be willing to step up and buy these 'toxic assets'?" Brother Tim was *right on* in his assessment. Yes indeed, any number of strong companies would have looked for an opportunity to profit and would have absorbed these assets for better or for worse. In fact, many did. For example, Bank of America bought Countrywide Home Loan and Merrill Lynch, and so on. That is how capitalism works. The best course of action that the U.S. federal government could have taken would have been to *do nothing, take absolutely no action whatsoever*. Instead, our elected leaders chose to make matters worse. They repeated the same mistakes of the 1930s by stepping in, throwing good money after bad money, and piling needless debt onto the backs of the American people. This will result in unnecessarily prolonging the pain.

> *"To contract new debts is not the way to pay old ones."*
> —**George Washington** to James Welch, April 7, 1799

---

*A personal story to illustrate this point…*I was fortunate enough to serve on the board of a community bank for more than a decade and learned a great deal from some very wise and successful people. John Benjamin Good led the bank that his grandfather founded in 1883. Ben was from "the Greatest Generation" and understood very well the importance of certain eternal concepts like honesty, trust, prudence, and good stewardship. What is even more important,

Ben *lived* those values every day of his life. Ben would *never* have been a party to creating a mess like we have now because he stuck to what worked. Ben stuck to fundamental principles that have worked for *all time*; principles like loaning money only to people who have the ability to repay the money and requiring that they have some "vested interest" in the form of a down payment, and so on. Ben understood that part of his job was to help keep people from getting into financial trouble. Sometimes, that meant protecting them from themselves. By that I mean protecting them from their own tendency to "overreach" financially or to pursue greed. Ben knew these actions could lead to disaster for them, for the bank, and for the depositors of the bank. Ben would not hesitate to remind loan officers, members of the loan committee, and bank board members that *"this is not our money, we are simply stewards."* Ben Good would not have "thrown good money at a bad loan." When there were bad loans, Ben took his losses and moved on, knowing that if you stick to the right principles in making loans, you won't have very many losses. Ben would say that when you do have losses, you should learn from them and accept them, but under no circumstance should you ever expect others to bail you out of your own bad decision. There is no doubt that if Ben Good were living today, he would be shocked and stunned at what the U.S. government is doing in response to this financial crisis. These current politicians need to be relieved of their duty and replaced before our great nation is damaged beyond repair.

"...You cannot spend your way out of a recession or borrow your way out of debt. And when you repeat, in that wooden and perfunctory way, that our situation is better than others, that we are well placed to weather the storm, I have to tell you, you sound like a Brezhnev era apparatchik giving the party line. You know and we know and you know that we know that it's nonsense. Everyone knows that Britain is worse off than any other country as we go into these hard times. The IMF has said so. The European Commission has said so. The markets say so, which is why the pound has lost a third of its value. In a few months, the voters will have their chance to say so, too. They can see what the markets have seen: that you are the devalued prime minister of a devalued government."
—**Daniel Hannan** to Prime Minister Gordon Brown on March 24, 2009
Daniel is a member of the European Parliament

"Man cannot make principles; he can only discover them."
—**Thomas Paine**, *The Age of Reason*, 1794

3. **What we are doing is un-American.** In #1 above, we reviewed why we can't afford what we are doing. In #2 above, we reviewed why what we are doing will not work. I would like now to provide you with what is perhaps the most important reason of all why you need to fight with every ounce of your strength against what our government is doing. ***It is un-American.*** What we are doing as a nation is counter to and goes against what made the United States the greatest nation to have ever existed. We do absolutely no one a favor and everyone a tremendous disservice by trying to "paper over" our own bad behavior. Besides, it is absolutely unfair, and yes un-American, to ask millions of average American taxpayers to pay for reckless mistakes made by a very few greedy, stupid, or unwise individuals. Oh, but the politicians will tell you that we can't let these banks and financial institutions fail, for it will cause a financial Armageddon in America. So what's their point? That is what capitalism is all about. With capitalism, there are winners and losers. We are going to have to take our medicine for these poor decisions sooner or later. Let's get it over with! Let the chips fall where they may. Sure, there will be pain but at least ***most*** of the pain will be visited upon those people and those institutions that ***deserve*** the pain. It is both interesting ***and sad*** how quickly we have forgotten what made this nation, the United States of America, the greatest economic powerhouse in the history of man. We have experienced ***many*** recessions and depressions in our nation's history. In each and every case, we have recovered and our economy has gone on to grow bigger and stronger than ever before. A true capitalistic system, if left alone, will heal itself remarkably fast. It is only when we attempt to intervene that we get ourselves into trouble and prolong the agony. The Great Depression of the 1930s is the best example of what ***not*** to do. That depression could have remained a recession if the U.S. government had not intervened with ***exactly the wrong measures***. Rather than spend time going into the evidence that proves this statement, I will refer you to a book titled ***The Forgotten Man*** by Amity Shlaes, which is available on Amazon.com. At the time this book is going to the publisher, the United States Speaker of the House of Representatives, Nancy Pelosi, has been characterizing the behavior of thousands of concerned American citizens as "un-American" because these folks have been showing up at town hall meetings with questions about the federal government's attempt to "take over" the entire health care delivery system in the United States. I would submit to you that the only folks who are un-American are people ***just like*** Nancy Pelosi. 170 years ago, Davey Crockett made this case better than I or anyone else could. So with that said, I would like to share with you ***a public story that proves my above claim that the recent action by the U.S. government is un-American:***

The "Not Yours to Give" Speech
Davey Crockett's View of the U.S. Constitution

David Crockett, *"King of the Wild Frontier"*
Born in Tennessee in 1786
Died at the battle of the Alamo in Texas on March 6, 1836

"We have the right, as individuals, to give away as much of our own money as we please in charity; but as members of Congress we have no right to appropriate a dollar of the public money".
—David Crockett, U.S. Congressman (1827-1835)

Everyone has heard the legend of Davey Crockett, an American folk hero, frontiersman, and soldier. But few know that he served as a U.S. Congressman from Tennessee from 1827 until 1835 before he gave his life defending Freedom at the Battle of the Alamo in 1836. The following excerpt, reprinted from an 1884 book with the title **_The Life of Colonel David Crockett_**, by Edward S. Ellis, illustrates the true meaning of the U.S. Constitution simply and elegantly. Davey Crockett understood what American government is all about—much better than today's self-serving, elitist, career politicians do.

One day in the U.S. House of Representatives, a bill was taken up appropriating money for the benefit of a widow of a distinguished naval officer. Several beautiful speeches had been made in its support. The Speaker was just about to put the question when Davey Crockett arose:

"Mr. Speaker, I have as much respect for the memory of the deceased, and as much sympathy for the sufferings of the living, if suffering there be, as any man in this House, but we must not permit our respect for the dead or our sympathy for a part of the living to lead us into an act of injustice to the balance of the living. I will not go into an argument to prove that Congress has no power to appropriate this money as an act of charity. Every member upon this floor knows it. We have the right, as individuals, to give away as much of our own money as we please in charity; but as members of Congress we have no right to appropriate a dollar of the public money. Some eloquent appeals have

been made to us upon the ground that it is a debt due the deceased. Mr. Speaker, the deceased lived long after the close of the war; he was in office to the day of his death, and I have never heard that the government was in arrears to him.

"Every man in this House knows it is not a debt. We cannot, without the grossest corruption, appropriate this money as the payment of a debt. We have not the semblance of authority to appropriate it as a charity. Mr. Speaker, I have said we have the right to give as much money of our own as we please. I am the poorest man on this floor. I cannot vote for this bill, but I will give one week's pay to the object, and, if every member of Congress will do the same, it will amount to more than the bill asks."

> Crockett took his seat. Nobody replied. The bill was put upon its passage, and, instead of passing unanimously, as was generally supposed, and as, no doubt, it would, but for that speech, it received but few votes, and of course, was lost.

Later, Crockett commented:

"There is one thing now to which I will call your attention. You remember that I proposed to give a week's pay. There are in that House many very wealthy men—men who think nothing of spending a week's pay, or a dozen of them, for a dinner or a wine party when they have something to accomplish by it. Some of those same men made beautiful speeches upon the great debt of gratitude which the country owed the deceased—a debt that could not be paid by money—and the insignificance and worthlessness of money, particularly so insignificant a sum as $10,000, when weighed against the honor of the nation. Yet not one of them responded to my proposition. Money with them is nothing but trash when it is to come out of the people. But it is the one great thing for which most of them are striving, and many of them sacrifice honor, integrity, and justice to obtain it."

David Crockett—

During the last third of our existence as a nation, most of our nationally elected leaders have demonstrated that they clearly lack an understanding **of** and an appreciation **for** the U.S. Constitution. This exceptional document has not changed since those days of Davey Crockett.

All that has changed has been our current elected leaders' willingness to abide by it. The time has arrived for us to meet our obligations in this regard. ***"We the People"*** are on shaky ground with respect to this issue. The consequences of our choosing to ignore the Constitution have brought us right up to the precipice of losing the very Republic for which it was written. Will you stand by and be a party to "*killing the goose that lays the golden eggs*"? ***Or*** will you stand up, be counted, get engaged, and choose a different course? The answer to these questions will be made known to all for a certainty on the 2nd day of November in 2010, when ***"We the People"*** vote in the next congressional elections. Meanwhile, based upon the recent protests all across America, I am encouraged that ***"We the People"*** are now starting to wake up.

> *"It is not the function of the government to keep the citizen from falling into error; it is the function of the citizen to keep the government from falling into error."*
> —Justice Robert H. Jackson

On National Health Care

We have this entire issue exactly backwards, completely upside down. We have forgotten who we are and what has made us so great as a nation. We must return to what works. We must have the courage to turn away from what we ***know*** does not work. Just this year in 2009, we saw our European friends turning away from socialism and transitioning back toward Freedom, Liberty, capitalism, and free enterprise. These are all of the principles upon which we were able to build our nation into the greatest economic miracle the world has ever witnessed. These principles are literally in our "national DNA." Why are we choosing to move away from these principles by nationalizing much of our private enterprise companies and industries? Shouldn't we be doing precisely the opposite? Shouldn't we be ***privatizing*** government-run entities such as the Post Office and Amtrak? Why don't we put the U.S. Post Office up for bid to successful companies like FedEx or UPS and sell Amtrak to successful privately held railroad companies? The behavior of our nation this past year makes absolutely no sense, given the history and experience of the United States. Our nation has clearly been hijacked by socialists.

As this is being written, ***"We the People"*** are in the process of debating the handover of the entire health care industry in the United States to a group of people who have proven beyond any reasonable doubt that they are completely and totally incapable of operating Social Security, Medicare, Medicaid, and legions of other programs on an efficient and profitable basis. The health care industry represents almost 20 percent of the entire U.S. economy, and yet we are about to turn it over to an entity that in 2008 *alone* allowed Medicare, Medicaid, and Social Security to be defrauded of an estimated $100 billion! What an indictment! Let us first allow the federal government to prove that they can be successful at something before we give them any new responsibilities, most especially the responsibility for something that comprises nearly 20 percent of the U.S. economy! What are we thinking? These people have created *$100 trillion* of financial liabilities that taxpayers of the United States are responsible to meet and have driven us into a national bankruptcy. The total federal government debt for our national liabilities now represent three hundred thousand dollars ($300,000) for *every man, woman, and child* in the United States or $1 million ($1,000,000) for *each and every household* in the United States. This type of insane behavior by our elected leaders on behalf of the American people needs to come to an abrupt end, not expanded into a whole new area!

The Obama administration early in 2009 began by estimating the cost to the American taxpayer for the takeover of the health care industry at around $650 billion. Democratic Representative Chris Van Hollen of Maryland appeared on "Fox News" on June 25, 2009, and said that the cost will likely exceed $1 trillion. According to the "U.S. House Discussion Draft" of June 19, 2009, the cost to taxpayers for national health care will be $3.5 trillion over ten years. Whether one is building a home or planning a project, we all know that the estimated cost for anything is always *low* as compared to the *actual final costs*. However, in the case of the United States nationalizing health care, it really doesn't matter whether the final cost will be $650 billion, $1 trillion, or $3.5 trillion *or more*. *"We the People"* cannot afford *ANY* amount of new spending or debt. What we seem to be forgetting is that *we are __BROKE!__* Is there any reason to point out that if we turn our health care over to the federal government that we are virtually guaranteed that the cost of health care will go way up and the quality and availability will precipitously drop? Need I say more? Probably not, for this issue falls under the category of Point #8, the "cease and desist order", of *__The 2ⁿᵈ American Revolution__* anyway. Point #8 is this: *"We the People"* do hereby put the United States Congress and the U.S. President on notice that they are to immediately *__cease and desist__* from any further "nationalization" of the private sector of the U.S. economy or intervention into the lives and property of *"We the People."*

On Compassion

What is compassion? Who are the compassionate among us? We would all agree that Mother Teresa was compassionate. Is compassion defined as 50 percent of people being enslaved to a life of servitude in order to support the other 50 percent of the people, who are enslaved to a life of dependency? If so, you define compassion as 50 percent of the population working very hard, producing lots of goods and services, making lots of money, and paying 50 percent or more of their income in taxes while the other 50 percent of the population work very little, produce relatively little, earn very little, and pay little or no taxes. <u>*Or*</u> is compassion defined as creating an environment in which people are *free* to pursue their own goals and dreams, succeed at a level of their own choosing, earn as little or as much as they want, pay as few or as many taxes as they choose? Which of our two major political parties would you say has more compassion? I would submit that *neither* of them fit the description. Your author prefers to define compassion as creating an environment in which people are *free* to pursue their own goals and dreams, succeed at a level of their own choosing, earn as little or as much as they desire, pay as few or as many taxes as they choose, and *be free* to help their fellow man. Your author believes that a life of enslavement, whether it is enslavement to a life of dependency or to a life of servitude, *is wrong*, yet that's the life we Americans are living today.

This quote by the late Adrian Rogers perfectly explains the concept of the "tipping point," which is the point at which the producers in a society become outnumbered in the voting booth by the non-producers. It is at this point in time when all democratic, capitalistic, free enterprise societies go into decline and ultimately disappear. These societies tend to last for a period on either side of 200 years, as explained below by Alexander Fraser Tytler (1747–1813). Would anyone like to hazard a guess where America stands on the 200-year timeline?

"You cannot legislate the poor into freedom by legislating the wealthy out of freedom. What one person receives without working for, another person must work for without receiving. The government cannot give to anybody anything that the government does not first take from somebody else.

"When half of the people get the idea that they do not have to work because the other half is going to take care of them, and when the other half gets the idea that it does no good to work because somebody else is going to get what they work for, that my dear friend, is about the end of any nation.

"You cannot multiply wealth by dividing it."

— **Dr. Adrian Rogers,** Southern Baptist minister, 1931–2005

John Adams was of the opinion that *"elections, especially of representatives and counselors, should be annual.... These great men ... should be [chosen] once a year — Like bubbles on the sea of matter bourne, they rise, they break, and to the sea return. This will teach them the great political virtues of humility, patience, and moderation, without which every man in power becomes a ravenous beast of prey."*

Abraham Lincoln humbly and candidly admitted, *"If our American society and United States government are overthrown, it will come from the voracious desire for office, this [desire] to live without toil, work, and labor ... from which I am not free myself."*

"Power tends to corrupt and absolute power corrupts absolutely."
—**Lord Acton,** 1887

"Governments destitute of energy, will ever produce anarchy."
—**James Madison**
Speech to Virginia Convention
June 7, 1788

"Rulers, surely, even the most dignified and powerful of them, should not be so elevated with the thoughts of their power, as to forget from whom it comes; for what purposes it is delegated to them."
—**Rev. Jonathan Mayhew**
(1720–1766) noted American clergyman and minister
Election Sermon, 1754

"When a man assumes a public trust, he should consider himself as public property."
— **Thomas Jefferson**
In a remark to Baron von Humboldt

Jonathan Mayhew
(Oct 8, 1720 to July 9, 1766) was a noted American clergyman and minister

A Thought-Provoking Story from the Time of Our Founding

The following has been attributed to Alexander Fraser Tytler (1747–1813), a Scottish-born lawyer and writer at about the time that our original thirteen states adopted their new Constitution in 1787; however, according to Snopes.com—www.snopes.com/politics/ballot/athenian.asp—it is unclear who actually authored the work.

The story is about the fall of the Athenian Republic some 2,000 years earlier:

> *A democracy is always temporary in nature; it simply cannot exist as a permanent form of government.*
>
> *A democracy will continue to exist up until the time that voters discover they can vote themselves generous gifts from the public treasury.*
>
> *From that moment on, the majority always vote for the candidates who promise the most benefits from the public treasury, with the result that every democracy will finally collapse due to loose fiscal policy, which is always followed by a dictatorship.*
>
> *The average age of the world's greatest civilizations, from the beginning of history, has been about 200 years.*
>
> *During those 200 years, the democratic nations always progressed through the following sequence:*
>
> > *1. From bondage to spiritual faith;*
> >
> > *2. From spiritual faith to great courage;*
> >
> > *3. From courage to Liberty;*
> >
> > *4. From Liberty to abundance;*
> >
> > *5. From abundance to complacency;*
> >
> > *6. From complacency to apathy;*
> >
> > *7. From apathy to dependence;*
> >
> > *8. From dependence back into bondage.*

To the reader: Your author has added the box and timeline below. It corresponds with the eight sequential time periods from above:

Where the United States of America fits on the above timeline:

1. Pilgrims arrive in Jamestown from Great Britain in 1607
2. People enjoyed religious freedom, became strong and courageous
3. Colonists fought and won their Freedom and Liberty (1775 to 1783)
4. The miracle of American capitalism from 1787 and beyond
5. Becoming fat, dumb, and happy in the latter half of the twentieth century
6. No longer caring about the gift of Freedom and taking it for granted
7. The welfare state and the beginning of socialism in America
8. Losing the gift of Freedom entirely and going back into a dictatorship

---

No matter the original source of the above work, it is both interesting and amazing how this pattern associated with the rise and fall of democracies seems to repeat itself. Can there be any doubt that our founders in their studies of the ancient societies had not discovered the same phenomenon? This would certainly explain their constant reminders to us of the need to never let down our guard against tyranny and to be constantly aware and mindful of the fragility of Liberty and Freedom. Where would you place America on the above timeline?

Your author estimates that we are somewhere between dependence and back into bondage. That puts us at about **7.5!** What are you willing to do about it? Are you willing to give up God's greatest gift to mankind—your Freedom and your Liberty?

Solutions:

1) Sell off the prime real estate of the United States and use the money to pay off our debt.
2) Move the activities from the prime real estate to other U.S. real estate in Nevada and Arizona.
3) *Eliminate* U.S. government programs and departments such as education, agriculture, labor, and so on.
4) Stop being the policeman of the world. Close fully half of our military bases and save billions.
5) Pass a Balanced Budget Amendment to the U.S. Constitution and a Presidential Line Item Veto.

Chapter Four
Federal Spending, Taxation, and the Sixteenth Amendment

1913—The Beginning of the End of Our American Republic

> *"The Congress shall have power to lay and collect taxes on incomes, from whatever source derived, without apportionment among the several States, and without regard to any census or enumeration."*
>
> —The Sixteenth Amendment to the U.S. Constitution, passed in 1913

Table 1 shows what happened to per capita (per person) spending by the U.S. federal government after the passage of the Sixteenth Amendment allowing the federal government to tax individuals on their incomes. Note the column on the right, which **"nets out"** spending on defense and interest on the debt. There was more than a *1,000%* (tenfold) increase in just twenty years! **Lesson: Give government the right to tax you, and they most certainly will do just that!**

Table 1: Real Per Capita Federal Expenditures: 1915–1935 (In Constant 1990 Dollars)		
Year	Total	Total Spending *Minus* Defense and Interest
1915	95.02	27.39
1916	83.60	22.75
1917	193.22	113.81
1918	1,067.31	518.37
1919	1,329.77	477.53
1920	390.98	170.15
1921	338.86	136.16
1922	232.95	78.62
1923	214.57	74.49
1924	194.85	70.36
1925	187.78	71.09
1926	184.80	76.57
1927	180.57	72.75
1928	186.56	79.89
1929	195.41	89.30
1930	211.13	101.81
1931	247.41	130.80
1932	286.39	183.98
1933	367.84	231.20
1934	498.88	361.02
1935	486.81	328.03

Source: *Historical Statistics of the United States from Colonial Times to 1970*, and author's calculations.

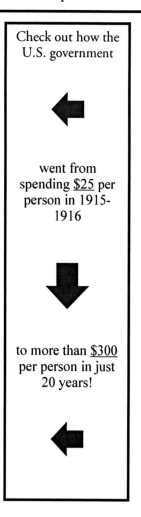

Check out how the U.S. government

went from spending <u>$25</u> per person in 1915-1916

to more than <u>$300</u> per person in just 20 years!

Would anyone like to take a guess how much that the federal government currently spends *per person* in 2009, net of defense and interest? Would you believe something close to *$10,000!?* And that's on 178 million *more people!* We had 128 million people in the United States in 1935, and we have 306 million people here in 2009! That's a *4,000* percent increase per person as compared to 1933; and a *40,000* percent increase per person as compared to 1916!

If the founding fathers had one overriding, primary mission when writing the U.S. Constitution, it was their desire to severely limit the power and scope of the central government. This was the one, single, solitary principle on which they **all** agreed. Even the Federalists, who favored a much stronger central government than did the other founders, understood the need to limit government's role. By 1787, everyone in the American colonies was quite ready to live their lives unencumbered by a tyrannical government. They all desired to be left alone and each earnestly believed that any power affecting the citizenry should be held at the *lowest possible level* in a society. Our founders also understood that the best decisions affecting people are made by the *family* or only at a very local level, where *accountability* would control. They studied the lessons that the past had to teach them from the societies of old (the Israelites, the Greeks, the Romans, and the Anglo-Saxons) and unanimously agreed that no good end would come from a strong central government making decisions for people from a faraway place. To put it in today's manner of speaking, they had *"been there and done that"* and were more than ready to move on.

The founders were so steadfast in their mission to restrict the central government that they literally starved their first central government under the Articles of Confederation of any financial means to fight the Revolutionary War. While they later remedied their error when they formed our current system of government under the U.S. Constitution, the founders still never wavered from their commitment to limit the influence over the people by the federal government. Slowly, but very *insidiously*, over the past hundred years, *"We the People"* have lost sight of the wisdom that our founders had in this regard and we have allowed the federal government to grow *exponentially*. One of the seminal events that can be pointed to where *"We the People"* clearly lost our way was in the passage in 1913 of the Sixteenth Amendment to our U.S. Constitution. That amendment granted vast power to the federal government to tax *each individual citizen*. Heretofore, the federal government had gotten the bulk of its resources from the various states. Under that arrangement, the states could control the growth and power of the central government. However, after 1913, under the new Sixteenth

Amendment, the federal government was then able to **bypass that state control** and **directly tax each individual citizen within those various states**. This change would serve from that day forward as a "blank check" on which the federal government would be allowed to grow unrestrained without any limits. This would ultimately lead to the federal government's ability to dominate and control the lives of each individual American. The very thing that our founders had worked so hard to avoid, and had actually feared the most, would now come to pass. Big decisions affecting the lives of people would no longer be made on a manageable local level by families, churches, and communities, so **accountability** could be maintained. Instead, they would be made in a faraway place by a **huge** federal bureaucracy. Your author believes that as a result of the Sixteenth Amendment, **we have become that which our founders feared most**.

The Oval Office, March 21, 1973

> *"I began by telling the President that there was a cancer growing on the presidency and that if the cancer was not removed, that the President himself would be killed by it. I also told him that it was important that this cancer be removed immediately because it was growing more deadly every day."*
> —**John Dean,** testifying before Congress in the Watergate Hearings June 25th, 1973

The above is John Dean's recitation of what he had told President Nixon in the Oval Office concerning the cover-up of the break-in to Democratic Headquarters at the Watergate Hotel in Washington, D.C. Dean was testifying before Congress during the Watergate Hearings just three months after his meeting with Nixon.

John Dean was President Nixon's personal attorney. The cancer that Dean refers to in the above quote was the cover-up that was occurring after the break-in to the Democratic Campaign Headquarters in Washington, D.C., by some "Nixon for reelection" operatives. John Dean's testimony and this analogy would become famous. Dean hoped that if he could be dramatic enough with Nixon in describing what was happening by covering up the break-in that Nixon might order all concealment efforts ended. Unfortunately for Nixon, and for America, Dean's attempt at drama failed, and ultimately President Nixon resigned from office for his participation in the Watergate cover-up. He resigned in order to avoid facing an almost certain impeachment proceeding which would very likely have removed him from office. This was a sad and extremely difficult time for our great nation.

Boy oh boy, our founders would have loved this guy:

> *"I heartily accept the motto `The government is best which governs least'; and I should like to see it acted up to more rapidly and systematically. Carried out, it finally amounts to this, which I also believe: `That government is best which governs not at all.'"*
>
> **—Henry David Thoreau,** 1817–1862

Government Is Like a Cancer

Why do I bring up John Dean's famous testimony from 1973? I bring it up because government is much like a cancer. Cancer is nothing more than cells that can't get organized and begin to grow exponentially, eventually killing the host on which it lives. Government, just like cancer, if allowed to grow exponentially and get large enough, will likewise eventually kill its host. The host on which government feeds is the nation's economic system, or the very nation itself. Government is an economic drag on an economy. The larger government spending becomes as a percentage of the gross domestic product (GDP), the bigger the drag on that economy. Allow government to grow unchecked, and like cancer, it will most assuredly overtake and, yes, __kill__ its host.

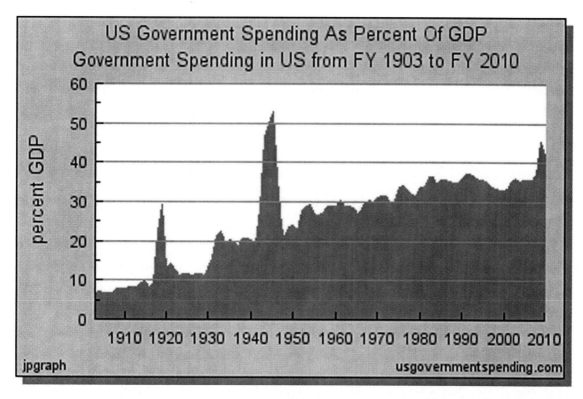

As you can see from the chart above, spending by the federal government as a percentage of the U.S. economy gradually grew from 6 or 7 percent of GDP to over 40 percent during the past 100 years (45 percent in 2009). Take note of the spikes for World War I, World War II, and the recent War on Terror. These "spikes" represent the spending that our founding fathers had in mind as being the "***single primary purpose***" for the U.S. federal government. Much more important than the spikes, please take note of the overall **_600 percent growth_** in government spending from around **_6 to 7 percent_** of GDP to currently **_45 percent_** in 2009. This is growth that our founders **_did not_** have in mind. In fact, it is what our founders feared most and had warned us repeatedly would happen if we were to let down our guard and not remain vigilant about keeping the size and scope of government small and manageable.

> "*The natural progress of things is for liberty to yield and government to gain ground.*"
> —**Thomas Jefferson** in a letter to Edward Carrington
> May 27, 1788

Where does government get the resources needed to function, if not from the people? The more resources the government is able to extract from the people, the larger and more powerful *it* becomes and the smaller and less powerful the *people* become. Our opportunity resides in our pain. We shall simply cut the feeding tube (the tax revenue) on which the beast grows and let the beast die. Otherwise, the beast will consume *"We the People."*

Reduce the Federal Government and Return Liberty and Freedom to *"We the People"*

Solutions: We *must* repeal the Sixteenth Amendment to the U.S. Constitution and, with it, the 66,000-page, IRS income tax code. Once we have eliminated or reduced in size large pieces of the federal government, it will not be necessary to replace the income tax as a source of revenue for the national treasury. The income tax comprises 40 to 45 percent of the revenue of the federal government. That is the approximate amount of the federal government that *"We the People"* will be eliminating or turning back to the people or to the states. Therefore, if there is a need for additional revenue for government, it will be for local or state governments, *not federal*. In that event, each state and local community will determine *on their own* whether they need any additional revenue. The consumption or sales tax that the fair tax people have proposed to replace the income tax on a national level has merit, and local governments within each state will likely consider it. This source of raising public revenue is appealing on many levels. Revenues are easy to collect—at the time of a purchase. Most states are now collecting revenue via this format anyway in the form of state sales taxes. The best feature of this source of tax revenue for government is that it discourages consumption by people and encourages thrift. Encouraging thrift in our nation will be essential and a great thing for the people in this new era as we transition from a debtor nation back to a creditor nation. An added bonus to all of this is that we will entirely eliminate the IRS's involvement in the lives of *"We the People."*

The important point here is that repealing the Sixteenth Amendment to the U.S. Constitution and eliminating the IRS, replacing it with a consumption tax, should *not* be done on a "national" basis with a "national" tax but rather with *each of the individual states and local communities* making these decisions on an *entirely "local"* level. History has clearly demonstrated, and we now know for a certainty, that any decisions affecting people on a personal basis *must* be made at the lowest possible level in the society so that *"accountability"* is possible and can be required. This will be a boon to America and give *"We the People"* great Freedom and Liberty to choose where we desire to live and how we choose to be governed. It will create an atmosphere in which *each person* can decide how much government involvement *they want* in their lives. If people desire that their government provide them more services, even including providing for their health care needs, they may choose to live in a state that provides a great array of state-run services and thereby pay a correspondingly high tax rate on their consumption. Likewise, if people desire a more limited governmental influence in their lives and choose to be more self-reliant, they can live in a state with low taxes and *be free* to provide services on their own. This system will create an environment in which states and communities will actually *compete* for where *"We the People"* live and work. It will generate efficiencies on a scale that would *never* be possible in a "one-size-fits-all" national system. This Federalism honors the original plan of our founders, and it also gives each individual American *tremendous* Freedom and Liberty. Just imagine; we will create a society in which all Americans have Freedom and Liberty that heretofore has been unimaginable.

While we are on this subject of taxes, let us set the record straight once and for all on this topic. If anyone doubts that less government and lower taxes are the answer to healing a sick economy, let them study recent history after the Kennedy and Reagan tax cuts of the 1960s and 1980s. These were administrations represented by both of the two major American political parties. Unfortunately, the positive effects of the Kennedy tax cuts were short lived thanks to L.B.J.'s massive spending on guns and butter (the Vietnam War and the explosion of welfare). While the Kennedy cuts were not nearly as dramatic as the Reagan tax cuts, they nevertheless were a big positive for the U.S. economy. The Reagan tax cuts were an altogether different story. They were much more aggressive and led to the largest and longest peacetime expansion of the American economy in U.S. history. "Reaganomics" worked *so well* that it resulted in literally millions of new jobs in the eighties and nineties. The Reagan economic revolution was so successful and became so *entrenched* in the U.S. economy that multiple attempts to kill it didn't work. George Bush's (41) tax increases of 1990 couldn't stop it. The massive Clinton tax hikes of 1993 couldn't even kill it. Reaganomics spawned the computer tech boom of the 1990s and ultimately brought about the fall of the Soviet Union's "evil empire," ending communism in most of the world. Reagan's pro-growth policies even led to the U.S. government's first balanced budget since 1957. Ronald Reagan simply followed what our founding fathers said to do, which was to provide for a strong defense of the nation and to stay out of the way of the people by reducing regulations and taxes. This wasn't rocket science; it was just being true to *genuine <u>American</u> ideals*. This all makes you wonder why it is often so difficult for people to see the overwhelming evidence that is placed right before them. Many politicians and economists argued at the time that Reaganomics wouldn't work. Reagan's vice president, George H.W. Bush (41), even coined a phrase to describe it as "voodoo economics" when he ran against Reagan in the primaries in 1980. Obviously we now have the advantage of history, which has ***proved Ronald Reagan was absolutely right.***

Okay, so we have just eliminated the income tax, thereby reducing the revenue to the federal government by 40 to 45 percent. We shall now discuss the specific changes needed in order to reduce the size and scope of the federal government.

Bold solutions to reduce the size and scope of the federal government under the *2nd American Revolution*:

Federal Spending Before and After the 2nd American Revolution

Specific Proposals for Cuts in Spending by the U.S. Federal Government:

Spending Category	2009 Spending	Proposed Cuts	Proposed 2014 Budget*	Comments
Social Security	$650 Billion	$50 Billion	$600 Billion	Fraud/administrative reductions.
Medicare	$400 Billion	$50 Billion	$350 Billion	Fraud/administrative reductions.
Defense Department	$650 Billion	$130 Billion	$520 Billion	Overall spending reduced 20%.
Medicaid	$250 Billion	$250 Billion	$ -0-	Will not exist on a national level.
Welfare/ Unemployment	$350 Billion	$350 Billion	$ -0-	Will not exist on a national level.
Interest on the Debt	$250 Billion	$150 Billion	$100 Billion	This cost will slowly go to $-0-.
Agriculture	$20 Billion	$20 Billion	$ -0-	Eliminate department entirely.
Education	$60 Billion	$60 Billion	$ -0-	Eliminate department entirely.
Energy	$25 Billion	$25 Billion	$ -0-	Eliminate department entirely.
Labor	$10 Billion	$10 Billion	$ -0-	Eliminate department entirely.
Housing	$35 Billion	$35 Billion	$ -0-	Eliminate department entirely.
All other spending	$400 Billion	$200 Billion	$200 Billion	50% minimum average** cuts
Totals	**$3.1 Trillion**	**$1.33 Trillion**	**$1.77 Trillion** *(all figures above are rounded.)*

*　For purposes of our comparisons, the 2014 proposed budget figures are assumed to be in constant 2009 dollars.

**　Some categories of spending under "all other" will be ***entirely eliminated***. ***All*** of the remaining categories will be reduced to varying degrees, resulting in an ***average minimum 50 percent*** reduction in spending in the "all other" areas.

As I have stated throughout this book, *the 2ⁿᵈ American Revolution* will not be about *"tinkering at the margins or nibbling at the edges"* of our national problems. We are left with no choice but to be **bold** and take very aggressive and decisive action in order to save our nation. Based on our past and current path of fiscal irresponsibility (with deficit spending now accelerating totally out of control), the only options that are available to *"We the People"* are the following:

1. Default on our debt
2. Inflate our way out of it by printing massive amounts of money thereby totally destroying our currency
3. Dramatically reduce the size and scope of the federal government of the United States of America

Choice 1 is not an option. The government will not default on our debt because honoring our debt obligations is our only means of convincing China and others to continue to loan us money. Choice 2 has been the policy of the United States government ever since we went off the gold standard in 1933 and began to print a "fiat" currency that was ***not*** backed by gold. Inflation is the "coward's way" out of honoring your obligations. Our inflation has been relatively moderate up to this point in time (with the exception of the late 1970s and early 1980s); however, with our recent levels of spending and debt accumulation, the only way to keep up will be to accelerate the printing of money and dramatically increase the money supply. This will result in creating *massive* hyperinflation. This inflation will debase and destroy our currency. The consequences of choice 2 will be that our creditors will stop loaning us money. Choice 1 is not an option and choice 2 will ***very soon*** become a non-option as well. Therefore, choice 3 is our only acceptable course of action if *"We the People"* choose to do the right thing and honor our obligations. It is also the *only* choice for us if *"We the People"* desire to save our nation and be true to our founders and forefathers.

What we have clearly learned over an extended period of time is that elitist career politicians are very definitely **not** the kind of people you want managing your affairs. They have operated Social Security as a gigantic Ponzi scheme for the past fifty years. There is no such thing as a Social Security "trust fund." Our elected leaders have spent all of the money that we have paid in Social Security taxes and as a consequence have **stolen** the future retirement income from you and millions of other American citizens. Bernie Madoff looks like a two-bit swindler when compared to our elected leaders in the U.S. Congress. We now need to relieve them all of their duties and find suitable replacements. The process of replacing them will begin in earnest on November 2, 2010 and will be complete in November, 2014 when the last group of the current U.S. Senators who are serving in office will be up for reelection. It is totally up to *"We the People"* as to whether we choose to repair our government or whether we allow our current bunch of corrupt elected leaders to finish ruining our nation. For patriotic Americans, this choice is an easy one. Throw them out and take back our Republic!

We will now review how the people and the states are to adjust to the above reductions in federal spending. Let us begin with welfare. If one were to set out to create the most inefficient way of helping people in need, it would be to do it through the federal government, where as much as 70 percent of welfare budgets get eaten up in waste and bureaucracy. On that basis, if *"We the People"* spend $600 billion on welfare and unemployment at the federal level each year, then families, churches, communities, and our local and state governments would only need to spend $180 billion on the ***direct*** benefits to recipients in order to have the ***same or better*** results. Best yet, even if we allow for 20 percent of funds collected at a local level to be used for administration and a ***local*** bureaucracy, *"We the People"* will need to be taxed at half ***or less*** at a ***local*** level to accomplish these ***same or better*** results. This alone will provide for a 50 percent tax cut for ***every*** American! Don't forget, we will no longer be paying any federal income tax. This approach assumes that *"We the People"* will begin taking more responsibility for ourselves once the federal government gets out of the welfare business. It is my firm belief that not only ***will we*** begin taking more individual responsibility for ourselves but that *"We the People"* actually ***want*** to do so. ***Below is a personal story that illustrates this point:***

My business partner, Jim Rea, and I were recently (June of 2009) in Boston, Massachusetts for meetings. We were at a Dunkin Donuts shop downtown having a breakfast sandwich and a cup of coffee one morning before starting our day. While seated there, an elderly gentleman walked in front of the store just outside the picture window where we were sitting. The gentleman looked disheveled, his clothes were soiled, his hair unkempt, and he was clearly struggling to make his way along. He was likely homeless. The man slowly made his way to the front door of the store and repeatedly looked inside and paced back and forth in front of the donut shop. Jim got up and went outside to speak with the man. The man held out his hand, in which he held a nickel and a dime. Jim asked him if he wanted something to eat. The man held forth his hand filled with the nickel and dime and nodded his head up and down, indicating that yes, he wanted something to eat. Jim invited the man into the store and asked him what he would like. The man asked for a breakfast sandwich and a cup of hot tea. Jim ordered the food for the man and proceeded down the line to pay the cashier. When Jim pulled out the money to pay for the man's food, the cashier said to him, *"No, don't worry about it; I will take care of it."* Jim offered once more to pay. Again, the lady said, *"No, I've got it."* The elderly homeless man and the lady cashier at Dunkin Donuts were of entirely different races. This true story clearly demonstrates that <u>*American*</u> kindness, generosity, and goodwill are alive and well today!

People feel better about themselves when they can be self-reliant. In the event people are unable to be self-reliant, for reasons that are beyond their own control, their fellow citizens in their *local community* feel good when they are able to help these less fortunate folks. In fact, they *want* to help. Once the cycle of poverty is broken, everyone will be much better off, and our national productivity will be greatly improved. Our founders had great compassion for the needy. However, they had the *wisdom* to know that caring for people out of the national treasury was not the way to help them and that it would lead to exactly what we have today which is graft, corruption, and a bloated federal bureaucracy. Our founders also knew that it was unfair, and many of them actually declared it un-American, to make these decisions on behalf of taxpayers. It is a crying shame that we have had to learn this lesson the hard way when we could have simply paid attention to what our founders and forefathers had to say on the matter. Rather than ending it abruptly, the plan will be to cut the federal welfare budget by a third each year for three years until it is entirely eliminated on the federal level. This will give adequate time for the people, their families, their churches, and communities as well as our local and state governments to adjust and to absorb this responsibility.

By the way, we also have the advantage of history on our side as a nation when it comes to proving the need to end welfare on a national basis. Even *if* providing transfer payments to individuals from the federal treasury were allowed under the U.S. Constitution, and please bear in mind that our U.S. Constitution in no way provides or allows for these transfer payments, *"The Personal Responsibility and Work Opportunity Reconciliation Act of 1996"* proves that there is no reason to continue them. A Democratic president, Bill Clinton, and a Republican Congress proved that welfare is not necessary when they undertook welfare reform in 1996. After this welfare reform act in 1996, people were required to go to work within two years of receiving benefits, and there was a lifetime cap of five years placed on benefits. In the aftermath, people fell off the welfare rolls in droves, became self-reliant, and began to feel much better about themselves. The success stories were legion. All societies will have poor people in them, and this will be the case **regardless** of how much money government or **"We the People"** spend on poverty. However, by providing for needy folks on a **local** level, and in a compassionate way, they will have a chance to become self-sufficient in a much shorter time due to accountability being available and manageable. This will break the perpetual and generational cycles of dependency that has plagued America since the very early days of the federal government's first attempts to help poor people. Thanks to President Clinton and the 104th Congress, we have now learned this national lesson.

The Department of Education should be among the first U.S. federal government departments to be entirely eliminated in our reorganization of the federal government. This entire episode in our history as a nation has been nothing short of a national embarrassment. The federal government didn't have any involvement whatsoever in the education of our children during the first 75 percent or so of our existence as a nation, and yet our children were **much better** educated in **those** days than they are in **our** day. One hundred years ago, the quality of education was much better than it is today. Several years ago, my business partner, George Huffman, showed me the final exam book that his father Lloyd (a teacher) gave his students when they graduated from the eighth grade. That particular exam was given in May of 1915, nearly one hundred years ago. George Huffman was born in 1920 and his father Lloyd was born in 1891. Below is a scanned image that includes a sampling of some questions from that exam:

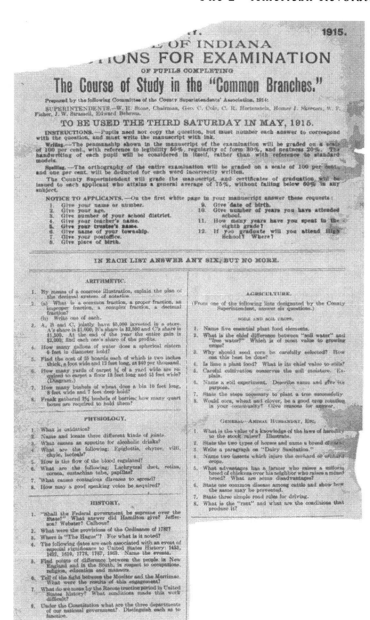

Please take note that this exam was given on a **Saturday.** The exam required the **entire day** to complete, as there was a morning and an afternoon set of questions. Based on items #11 and #12 of the "NOTICE TO APPLICANTS" in the rules section at the beginning of the exam, there was no guarantee that anyone would pass the exam. Evidence of this is clear in question #11—"__*How many years have you spent in the eighth grade?*__" and in #12—"*If you graduate, will you attend high school? Where?*" Wow! Obviously the concept of providing "social" promotion had not been thought of a hundred years ago, for it was clearly expected from these questions that some of the students would be attending eighth grade for more than just one year.

It is also quite clear from this exam that Americans a hundred years ago were **very** serious about educating their children. I would submit that it would be a daunting challenge in today's America for any twelfth grade student graduating from high school or perhaps even a college senior to pass this exam! These folks didn't need any federal guidance or assistance in order to educate children. It is abundantly clear from this **one** example that **local** township trustees who lived in the **local** community and were therefore directly **accountable** to the parents of the students did just fine in educating children! Your author believes that this is precisely the type of public education system to which America needs to return.

Now we know why an eighth grade education was considered adequate in America 100 years ago. These young folks were very adequately prepared to face the real world once they had mastered these subjects!

Below are some random test questions from the above Eighth Grade Exam:

Arithmetic: How many gallons of water does a spherical cistern six feet in diameter hold?

Physiology: What are the following: Lachrymal duct, retina, cornea, Eustachian tube, and papillae?

History: Shall the Federal Government be supreme over the State? What answer did Hamilton give? Jefferson? Webster? Calhoun?

Agriculture: Name five essential plant food elements.

Grammar: Compare and contrast the adjective and adverb, noun and pronoun, preposition and conjunction.

Geography: Name the kind of government found in each of the following countries: Germany, United States, Portugal, Japan, China, Brazil, Canada, France, Italy, Turkey

Reading: In the drama of *Julius Caesar*, are your sympathies with Caesar or his enemies? Why?

Industrial Arts: What is meant by joints in woodwork? Name two kinds of joints and tell how each is made.

Music: What is the use of Sharps? Flats?

Domestic Science: What is a simple test for fresh eggs?

Indiana History: Give an accounting of Abraham Lincoln's life in Indiana.

Civics: Why do we have courts? Why do we have legislatures?

Art: Make a pencil sketch suitable for use on an Easter card.

Cooking: What causes the spoiling of fruits, vegetables, and meals?

Household management: Why should the mother and father be members of community organizations?

While we are on this subject of education, let's consider "home-schooling" for a moment. Over mostly the past three decades, millions of Americans became fed up with the mediocrity of the public school system. As a result, parents began teaching their children at home. My brother Tim and his wife Annalynn have five children ranging from twelve to twenty-five years of age. Annalynn has home-schooled each one of these children during the majority of their primary education years (grades kindergarten through twelfth). Below are the results of those efforts:

Danielle, the eldest, now twenty-five, holds a bachelor's and a master's degree in occupational therapy.

Lauren, now twenty-three, holds an engineering degree from Notre Dame and is finishing her law degree.

Nicola, twenty-one, is a senior at Notre Dame finishing her bachelor's degree in chemical engineering.

I believe the odds are excellent that the two younger ones, Thomas and James, will likewise flourish.

Could there be any possibility that their mother Annalynn's efforts on behalf of these children had a positive influence on the success of their outstanding educational outcome? While statistical proof might not be possible, I would pin my hopes and put my money on the efforts of Annalynn and millions of other parents just like her. It is important to note that most of our founding fathers were very highly educated men. Do you know what is also common about most of them? Most of them were to a great extent "home-schooled." George Washington, father of our country, was home-schooled. Benjamin Franklin, the fifteenth of seventeen children and America's most celebrated inventor and thinker, was *entirely* home-schooled. Thomas Jefferson was afforded a formal education by virtue of his father leaving funds at his death (Jefferson's father died when Thomas was age fourteen) for the express purpose of educating him. Jefferson was known to study for fifteen hours per day. While he was not one of our founding fathers, Abraham Lincoln was almost entirely self-taught. Lincoln had an insatiable desire to learn, and this lasted throughout his entire life.

A prime example illustrating the mistake of making decisions about educating children from a remote place can be found right in your own backyard. In the 1960s, the state of Indiana made the *less-than-brilliant* decision to consolidate school districts county-by-county. The result was that children spent much of their day on a school bus (where they learned things that would have been better saved for an older age), were placed in classrooms with many more students in them than was conducive to a quality education and learning, and were treated more like numbers than people. This change also created an environment in which parents had greater difficulty being actively involved in their children's education. Incidents of drug use and teenage pregnancy skyrocketed. When schools were consolidated, much of the "sense of community" was forever lost in many small towns throughout America. I was a product of this

Indiana school consolidation and can therefore attest that ***very little*** from Lloyd Huffman's "fundamental subjects" of 1915 above were taught in Indiana public schools in the 1960s and 1970s. In addition, I can tell you from first-hand personal experience that school consolidation turned out to be an overall unmitigated disaster for the quality of education in Indiana.

Chapter Five
Term Limits for the U.S. Congress
February 27, 1951—A Good Start

Twenty-second Amendment to the U.S. Constitution

"No person shall be elected to the office of the President more than twice, and no person who has held the office of President, or acted as President, for more than two years of a term to which some other person was elected President shall be elected to the office of the President more than once..."

March 21, 1947—Presidential Term Limits passed in the U.S. Congress
February 27, 1951—Final ratification by the states and becomes law

---

The Twenty-second Amendment to the U.S. Constitution was passed by the U.S. Congress on March 21, 1947, and was ratified by enough states (75 percent) to become law on February 27, 1951. Franklin D. Roosevelt made the passage of the Twenty-second Amendment necessary when he violated the long-held tradition of a two-term limit begun by our first president, George Washington, and honored by the next thirty presidents who followed Washington from the very beginning of our nation's existence. Roosevelt campaigned for and won not one, not two, not three, but four terms to the U.S. presidency. Upon his death in 1945, it became immediately clear that we could never do this again. Thousands of young adults had grown up as children and passed well into adulthood never having known any president other than F.D.R. There was an entire generation of people at the time who truly had come to believe the nation itself would come to an end now that President Roosevelt had died. This event was widely viewed as dangerous for our nation. Thomas Jefferson wrote the following in 1807 regarding presidential term limits:

"If some termination to the services of the chief Magistrate be not fixed by the Constitution, or supplied by practice, his office, nominally four years, will in fact become for life..."

Thomas Jefferson in 1807

Thomas Jefferson had no way to know that his prediction would literally become reality, for Roosevelt would die in office! Why didn't our founders address this in the U.S. Constitution? We may never have a clear answer to this question but thankfully the founders did provide an avenue for us to amend the document; and so we did.

Thomas Jefferson not only respected and honored the tradition first set by George Washington, on voluntarily limiting the terms of the U.S. presidency to just two, he also knew that we should limit the terms of Congress. In this statement, Jefferson is clearly **_not_** limiting his comments to just the terms of the U.S. presidency.

"To prevent every danger which might arise to American freedom from continuing too long in office, it is earnestly recommended that we set an obligation on the holder of that office to go out after a certain period."
—**Thomas Jefferson**

It seems that we have come full circle in the two hundred years between 1807 and 2009. Our nation's original Constitution did not provide for **any** form of term limits on any federal office. Despite this, our founders as well as the leaders who followed for the next more than a hundred years held to a tradition of **voluntarily** limiting their time in office. Then in the early part of the twentieth century, elected leaders began to ignore the tradition until Franklin D. Roosevelt's actions of seeking and winning four terms to the U.S. presidency resulted in the passage and the ratification of the Twenty-second Amendment to the U.S. Constitution, which is shown and described above. *"We the People"* now need to force the same limitations on our other federal officials in the U.S. Congress.

President Obama for Life?

The above banner is taken from Rep. Serrano's Web site: www.serrano.house.gov

We now find ourselves at a very dangerous point in our history in which a U.S. congressman from the state of New York has sponsored legislation that would repeal the Twenty-second Amendment to the U.S. Constitution. This is scary stuff. Representative Jose Serrano on January 6, 2009, filed the following legislation in the Congress:

HJ 5 IH   **111th CONGRESS, 1st Session**

H. J. RES.

Proposing an amendment to the Constitution of the United States to repeal the Twenty-second article of amendment, thereby removing the limitation on the number of terms an individual may serve as President.

IN THE HOUSE OF REPRESENTATIVES
January 6, 2009

Mr. SERRANO introduced the following joint resolution; which was referred to the Committee on the Judiciary.

JOINT RESOLUTION

Proposing an amendment to the Constitution of the United States to repeal the Twenty-second article of amendment, thereby removing the limitation on the number of terms an individual may serve as President.

Resolved by the Senate and House of Representatives of the United States of America in Congress assembled (two-thirds of each House concurring therein), That the following article is proposed as an amendment to the Constitution of the United States, which shall be valid to all intents and purposes as part of the Constitution when ratified by the legislatures of three-fourths of the several States within seven years after the date of its submission for ratification:

Article—

'The Twenty-second article of amendment to the Constitution of the United States is hereby repealed.'

So there you have it—President Obama, or some future president, ***for life***. Scary, isn't it? There is no need to panic quite yet. Amending the Constitution requires a two-thirds (2/3) majority vote in both houses of Congress to pass and then an additional hurdle of three fourths (3/4) of the states to ratify it before the law can go into effect. Nevertheless, this is an ominous sign of the mentality of at least one so-called representative of the people who is currently leading our great nation. This action in early 2009 makes it all the more urgent that ***"We the People"*** act on requiring that a Term Limits Amendment be passed by Congress and ratified by the States. You will read at the end of this chapter that it is well within the power of ***"We the People"*** to accomplish this.

---

*"**Nothing so strongly impels a man to regard the interest of his constituents, as the certainty of returning to the general mass of the people from whence he was taken, where he must participate in their burdens.**"*
—**George Mason** (1725–1792)
June 17, 1788, Speech in the Virginia Ratifying Convention

Founding father who, along with James Madison,
is considered the "Father of the Bill of Rights"

James Madison

"All men having power ought to be mistrusted."
—**James Madison** Fourth President of the United States of America, 1809 to 1817

"All power in human hands is liable to be abused."
—**James Madison**, December 18, 1825

Considered by many to be the *"Father of the Constitution"*
Also considered by many to be the
"Father of the Bill of Rights"

A New Push for a Term Limits Amendment to the U.S. Constitution

A Term Limits Amendment to the U.S. Constitution limiting the number of terms in office that our U.S. House and Senate federal officials may serve is much needed and is long overdue. The effort to bring about this change should not, ***and must not***, be further delayed. Given the way in which we operate the U.S. government, one could easily argue that the sum total of what we have accomplished these past 250 years has been to simply replace one set of royalty on the far side of the Atlantic with a new oligarchy on the East Coast of our own homeland. Our current career political system virtually guarantees that little to nothing of any real substance for the good of the nation will occur in government. Not one of our elected officials will risk losing the next election if it means going out on a limb and proposing that we actually begin to behave rationally on fiscal issues or that we actually secure our borders. It should be no surprise that our national legislature can't get anything meaningful accomplished, for there are no *"fresh ideas"* to be found in Washington, D.C. The United States is plagued with corrupt, elitist, career politicians who are more interested in staying in power and lining their own pockets than in justly and honorably serving this great nation of ours. These politicians are more beholden to lobbyists and special interest groups than they are to the folks back home. We need to broom them all from office and start over.

Most Americans agree that our current system of selecting elected federal officials is broken. The opinion of this farmer from Indiana (and by the way, it is also the opinion of more than 80 percent of the U.S. population) is that we desperately need to amend the Constitution of the United States to require that term limits be placed on people serving in the U.S. Congress. This is the only way that we can protect our elected officials from *"themselves"* by eliminating the desire to win an office solely for the dual purposes of personal financial gain and self-aggrandizement. Our goal should be to design the final result so that the system will attract ***only*** those Americans who are running for office to serve for the ***right*** reasons, those reasons being to selflessly serve their nation and their constituents back home. This is an essential step if we are going to be able to once and for all solve the serious problems that confront our nation. We need the involvement of ***new people*** with ***fresh ideas***. With ***"term limits done right,"*** we will once again enjoy the true *"representative"* government that our founders worked so hard to create for us instead of what we have evolved into, which is a "perpetual royal oligarchy" made up of the same old people with their old, stale, and worn-out ideas. Unfortunately, in today's world, we do not have the same high caliber of people we had at the beginning of our nation's founding and up through Abraham Lincoln's time. People during these early days of our nation were willing to seek office for the noblest of reasons, and that is ***sadly*** not the case today. Due to this change, term limits have now become a ***necessity***.

Abraham Lincoln

Sixteenth President of the
United States of America
Born 1809—Died 1865

As you read earlier in this book, Abraham Lincoln ran for the U.S. House of Representatives in 1846 and won a two-year term. At that time, there was an understanding that, if elected, a person would serve one term and then go home and back to work in the "real world". This was a long-standing tradition from the very beginning of our nation, and it made room for many others to serve their country. Despite the fact that he loved the job and would very likely have been reelected, Lincoln honored the long-held tradition of the time and did not even seek a second term. Unfortunately, as evidence of the past century has proven, a noble attitude like this by the politicians of today is just too much to expect in the reality of our current world. It is interesting to note that the sentiment of stepping aside and allowing others to serve actually reached its peak right at the time Lincoln served in the U.S. House of Representatives. See the chart below to learn more about what has transpired over the course of our history as respects the reelection rates of members of the U.S. Congress:

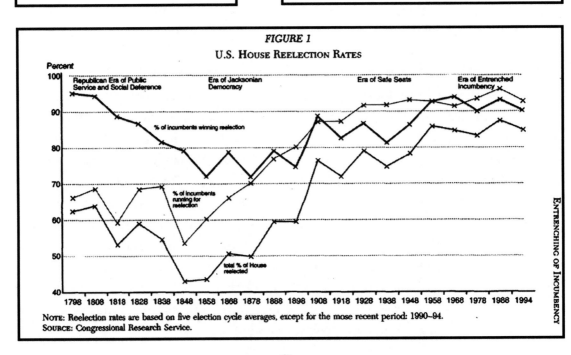

FIGURE 1
U.S. HOUSE REELECTION RATES

Note: Reelection rates are based on five election cycle averages, except for the most recent period: 1990–94.
Source: Congressional Research Service.

Some Interesting as Well as Disturbing Facts:

1. In November of 2004, of the 401 incumbent U.S. House members who sought reelection, *ALL* but **five** were reelected. That equates to a **_99_** percent reelection rate for members of the U.S. House of Representatives!

2. In November of 2004, of the twenty-six incumbent U.S. Senate members who sought reelection, *ALL* but **one** were reelected. That equates to a **_96_** percent reelection rate for members of the U.S. Senate!

3. As of January 20, 2006, *over **40*** percent of the members of the U.S. House and Senate had served for ***more than thirty years***. That means **_224_** members of the U.S. Congress holding office for more than *thirty* years!

4. In 2008, a candidate challenging an incumbent U.S. Senator was ***outspent by that incumbent an average*** of over **$7,500,000**. A candidate challenging an incumbent U.S. House member was ***outspent by that incumbent an average*** of over **$1,000,000**.

5. The current salary for the majority of the members of Congress is $174,000 per year to compensate them for their three-day workweek. This fact puts these people in the ***top 5 percent*** of all incomes in the United States.

6. The current salary for the Speaker of the House of Representatives is $223,500 per year.

7. The current salary for the President of the United States is $400,000 per year.

8. Lobbyists spend roughly an astounding ***$5 million per member*** of Congress each year to sway those members of Congress toward voting in favor of any number of the lobbyists' special interests.

9. ***Each*** member of the U.S. Congress has from fourteen to eighteen staff people and spends between ***$1.3 and $1.6 million*** each year just on expenses related to running their office.

10. The U.S. Congress voted themselves ***an additional $93,000 each*** in petty cash in January of 2009!

11. On average, over the last nine years, Congress has met about 140 days during each calendar year.

<u>As to #1 and #2 above</u>: If the politicians we are electing are financially driving our nation into the ground, why do they keep getting reelected at these obscene rates of more than 95 percent? It is because they get to choose who votes for them. It is called gerrymandering, a system that allows congressional districts to be redrawn at the whim of the politicians. Under this system, politicians essentially can pick and choose who they want to represent. As a result of this,

congressional districts look more like a scribble on the map by a three-year-old than the neat and tidy blocks of districts that you and I would draw. The two aims of gerrymandering are to maximize the effect of supporters' votes and to minimize the effect of opponents' votes. It is done to favor <u>incumbent</u> politicians. While the federal government outlawed "redlining" (the practice of discriminating by geographic area) to avoid discrimination in the Fair Housing Act of 1968, the same people who passed that law don't seem to mind using discrimination when designing their congressional districts so that they can "segregate" people by racial minorities, ethnic groups, and so on when it is to their advantage in getting reelected. Did someone say hypocrite? See below (from Wikipedia) two examples of gerrymandered districts.

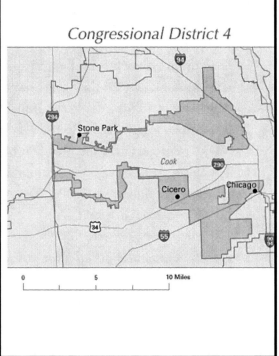

Printed in 1812, this political cartoon illustrates the electoral districts drawn by the Massachusetts legislature to favor the incumbent Democratic-Republican Party candidates of Governor Elbridge Gerry over the Federalists, from which the term "gerrymander" is derived. The cartoon depicts the bizarre shape of a district in Essex County, Massachusetts, as a dragon. The painter, Gilbert Stuart, likened it to a salamander, and the editor, Benjamin Russel, advised, "Better say a Gerrymander." The name stuck.
This is from Wikipedia.

The earmuff shape of Illinois's 4th Congressional district connects two Hispanic neighborhoods while remaining contiguous by narrowly tracing Interstate 294.
This is from Wikipedia.

As to #3 and #4 above: The United States Congress has forty members who have been serving for more than forty years, and there are a handful of them who have been there more than fifty years! What **"We the People"** have is an **aristocracy** running our country. Is it any wonder that we don't have the new ideas that are needed to solve our nation's problems? Have you ever considered why we can't seem to get the caliber of people to run for office that we could really get excited about voting for—like honest, hard-working, patriotic people? Or maybe some businesspeople who are able to understand and repair our financial problems? It is because entrenched career elitist politicians lock them out of the system! This must change. Term limits are the solution to this one.

As to #5, #6, and #7 above: During the first **158 years** of the United States, members of Congress received pay of around $1,000 per year in the very beginning, and it never exceeded $10,000 in those first **158** years. Over the past sixty years, compensation has rapidly grown to now $174,000 **plus** pensions and other special benefits. George Washington refused to accept **any** compensation whatsoever during the eight years that he served as commander in chief during the Revolutionary War. When the Constitution was adopted, it called for an annual salary for the President of $25,000. George Washington also refused the $25,000. Please understand that Washington didn't refuse the pay because it wasn't needed. Fighting the Revolution had left him in **great** need of money. Many of our founders considered it beneath their dignity to receive compensation of any kind to serve their nation. They felt it was their **duty** to serve and many were offended if offered compensation. <u>**Wow**</u>, how times have changed.

As to #8, #9, #10, and #11 above: There are **insane** amounts of money sloshing around our elected leaders. It is no wonder politicians leave office as multimillionaires, no matter their station in life when they first took office. This all needs to be outlawed, and there is a very simple and unique way of accomplishing that goal. Details will follow at the end of this chapter under Solutions. Meanwhile, let's continue our term limits discussion.

"Society in every state is a blessing, but government, even in its best state, is but a necessary evil; in its worst state, an intolerable one." —**Thomas Paine**, *Common Sense*, 1776

Some newly elected representatives can still see the forest for the trees. Let's have some more new ones in 2010!

> *"Today's federal government is too big, too powerful, and too expensive because it is doing things beyond the scope of the Constitution. This is foolish and it is dangerous."*
>
> **Dr. Paul Broun** is a newly elected (in 2007) U.S. House Representative from Georgia

<u>What Form Should Term Limits Take?</u>

There are many ways to argue what *form* term limits should take, and there are a multitude of combinations that might be appropriate. However, there is only *one* decision to make when considering *whether* or not we need them. That decision is answered by a simple *yes*. Because more than 80 percent of the American people are now in favor of term limits, we most assuredly know that we should have them. Therefore, perhaps it is really of no great concern what final form term limits will take. It may be likely that most reasonable people would agree that no one person should be allowed to serve longer than twelve years in any federal office. If that is agreed to, the final form the amendment takes is really unimportant. The important thing is that we pass the Constitutional Amendment, and it finally appears that our country is now ready for that result. What form do you believe term limits should take? Do we limit the U.S. Congress to two terms for both the House and Senate (four years for the House and twelve for the Senate), just like the presidency? Do we go with eight years total to match the limit of the President's years in office by changing both the Senate and House terms to four years? Perhaps we should just change the House terms to four years. This would allow elected officials more time to get things done and not exhaust the candidates with nonstop election cycles. Terms could be rotated so that we continue our two-year election cycle. This would also allow us to provide for the constant flow of *"fresh ideas"* that we so desperately need. It also seems reasonable and prudent that candidates not be allowed to run for any *new* office while they are serving in their current one. Too much time is wasted on the campaign trail. The result is that the elected officials are *not "serving"* in their *current* office. This really creates a form of "<u>theft</u>" from the American people. Once anyone has served two terms in one national office, they should not be allowed to run for any other office, except perhaps if we have a real statesman on our hands and that person desires to compete for the presidency.

We've Been Here Before

In 1994, the Republican Party ran on a platform during the mid-term elections called the "Contract with America." Their "contract" detailed ten specific action items that Congress would undertake if the election resulted in a Republican Party victory large enough to wrest control away from the Democrats. Included among those ten items was an ***amendment to the U.S. Constitution*** that would have imposed twelve-year term limits on members of the U.S. Congress (i.e., six terms for Representatives, two terms for Senators). It was passed by the U.S. House in a 227–204 vote but failed to meet the Constitutional Amendment requirement of a two-thirds majority (instead of a simple majority). The measure therefore went down in defeat. What we learned from this experience is that when it comes right down to it, ***our elected officials of today do not have the courage to vote themselves out of office. "We the People"*** are therefore left with no option but to do it for them.

Keep in mind that it is not easy to amend the Constitution of the United States, and the process takes time. In many cases, five years or more have gone by between the time that an amendment is passed by Congress and ultimately ratified by the required number of states. The founders purposely made it difficult to amend the U.S. Constitution. They did not want our Constitution to be easily changed at the whim of a simple majority of legislators. The founders required a two-thirds (2/3) majority of the U.S. Congress to agree to any change in the Constitution. Once that hurdle is met, three-fourths (3/4) of the states have to vote in favor of the act of Congress in order to ratify the amendment. The founders wanted to make certain that there was an overwhelming need for a change and that a great majority of the people were in favor of such a change. So, if our current U.S. House and U.S. Senate officials are unwilling to do the right thing in passing a Term Limits Amendment to the U.S. Constitution, this begs the question: ***How are we ever going to be able to accomplish the task?*** It seems that we are in a sort of "Catch-22." The solution is really quite simple and can actually be accomplished in the ***2010*** election cycle. All that is required is that ***"We the People"*** simply need to elect enough new members to Congress who are willing to make the change. And just how do we accomplish that feat? Next is where we begin to offer the solutions.

"*Experience should teach us to be most on our guard to protect liberty when the government's purposes are beneficent...the greatest dangers to liberty lurk in insidious encroachment by men of zeal, well-meaning but without understanding.*"

— **Justice Louis Brandeis,** 1856 to 1941
He served as Justice to the United States
Supreme Court from 1916 to 1939

Solution to amending the U.S. Constitution putting in place term limits for the Congress:

Prior to the 2010 mid-term elections, a grass-roots movement is begun to encourage all of the electorate in the United States to vote *only* for candidates who are *new* to office <u>*and*</u> who are willing to commit to vote in favor of a Term Limits Amendment to the Constitution. We have two opportunities in 2010 to make this happen. The first opportunity is during the primary elections. Voters should vote *only* for a candidate in the primary who is in favor of and pledges to support a Term Limits Amendment. Of necessity, this will require voting against *all* incumbents. The second opportunity is during the general election in November of 2010. Once again, voters should vote only for a candidate who is in favor of and pledges to support a Term Limits Amendment. Again, this will mean that we *must* vote the current officeholder (incumbent) out of office, as they have demonstrated in the recent past their unwillingness to pass such an Amendment. It will take a concerted effort by a large percentage of voting Americans, but it can be done. In fact, it must be done if we are to honor the sacrifice of our founders by restoring true representative government.

Solutions to bringing a competitive environment and ethics to the election process:

Once *"We the People"* have elected a new **"people's"** Congress, they will then have a mandate to:

1. Pass a Term Limits Amendment to the U.S. Constitution and send it to the States for ratification.

2. Reset the Congressional districts on a simple and fair basis and outlaw gerrymandering forever.

3. Outlaw lobbying entirely and, along with it, fundraising by political candidates or political parties. This will create a level playing field for all candidates who wish to run for elective office. The public will finance all campaigns out of the treasury for Congress and the Presidency. Debates will be held on public television during a series of evenings, and candidates can make their case.

4. The new **"people's"** Congress shall do a top-to-bottom review of compensation for the Congress, how much time they spend in their home districts, the size of their staffs, their budgets, and so on. Certainly an end should be made to any pensions for members of Congress, as it will be unlawful for them to serve for a length of time that would entitle them to any retirement. Besides, the goal is to attract **"citizen"** statesmen who desire to serve their country out of a sense of duty, and not out of any motivation involving financial gain. ***We are changing the emphasis***. In this way, we will attract an entirely "new and different" public servant than we have in the recent past. As we "elevate the process," we will begin to attract true Patriots, people who up to this point have been unwilling to step forward due to their high ethical standards and refusal to compromise their long held values. ***It is the firm belief of your author that these American Patriots are out there, just waiting for an opportunity to help restore the principles and values of our founding fathers.***

5. Begin the immediate elimination of many federal departments and their programs as well as begin dismantling the federal welfare state, evolving it back to individuals, families, local and state governments. Begin selling off and liquidating much of the valuable real estate held by the U.S. federal government and use the sale proceeds to pay down the United States national debt.

6. Pass amendments to the U.S. Constitution for a balanced budget and a presidential line item veto. Having narrowly escaped a financial Armageddon that would have

led to the very demise of our great nation, we now need an abundance of caution to make certain that we never again face the same risks to our nation's future. Requiring a balanced budget by the federal government will provide the security we need going forward. The only exception to this amendment will be in the event of war. Only Congress is empowered to declare war. And no more passing the buck to the President! A presidential line item veto will work hand in glove with the balanced budget.

7. Amend the Constitution to limit Supreme Court Justices and other federal judges to a 9-year term.

Declaration of Independence

Here is the complete text of the Declaration of Independence.
The original spelling and capitalization have been retained.
(Adopted by Congress on July 4, 1776)

The Unanimous Declaration
of the Thirteen United States of America

When, in the course of human events, it becomes necessary for one people to dissolve the political bonds which have connected them with another, and to assume among the powers of the earth, the separate and equal station to which the laws of nature and of nature's God entitle them, a decent respect to the opinions of mankind requires that they should declare the causes which impel them to the separation.

We hold these truths to be self-evident, that all men are created equal, that they are endowed by their Creator with certain unalienable rights, that among these are life, Liberty and the pursuit of happiness. That to secure these rights, governments are instituted among men, deriving their just powers from the consent of the governed, that whenever any form of government becomes destructive to these ends, it is the right of the people to alter or to abolish it, and to institute new government, laying its foundation on such principles, and organizing its powers in such form, as to them shall seem most likely to effect their safety and happiness. Prudence, indeed, will dictate that governments long established should not be changed for light and transient causes; and accordingly all experience hath shown that mankind are more disposed to suffer, while evils are sufferable, than to right themselves by abolishing the forms to which they are accustomed. But when a long train of abuses and usurpations, pursuing invariably the same object, evinces a design to reduce them under absolute despotism, it is their right, it is their duty, to throw off such government, and to provide new guards for their future security. --Such has been the patient sufferance of these colonies; and such is now the necessity which constrains them to alter their former systems of government. The history of the present King of Great Britain is a history of repeated injuries and usurpations, all having in direct object the establishment of an absolute tyranny over these states. To prove this, let facts be submitted to a candid world.

He has refused his assent to laws, the most wholesome and necessary for the public good.

He has forbidden his governors to pass laws of immediate and pressing importance, unless suspended in their operation till his assent should be obtained; and when so suspended, he has utterly neglected to attend to them.

He has refused to pass other laws for the accommodation of large districts of people, unless those people would relinquish the right of representation in the legislature, a right inestimable to them and formidable to tyrants only.

He has called together legislative bodies at places unusual, uncomfortable, and distant from the depository of their public records, for the sole purpose of fatiguing them into compliance with his measures.

He has dissolved representative houses repeatedly, for opposing with manly firmness his invasions on the rights of the people.

He has refused for a long time, after such dissolutions, to cause others to be elected; whereby the legislative powers, incapable of annihilation, have returned to the people at large for their exercise; the state remaining in the meantime exposed to all the dangers of invasion from without, and convulsions within.

He has endeavored to prevent the population of these states; for that purpose obstructing the laws for naturalization of foreigners; refusing to pass others to encourage their migration hither, and raising the conditions of new appropriations of lands.

He has obstructed the administration of justice, by refusing his assent to laws for establishing judiciary powers.

He has made judges dependent on his will alone, for the tenure of their offices, and the amount and payment of their salaries.

He has erected a multitude of new offices, and sent hither swarms of officers to harass our people, and eat out their substance.

He has kept among us, in times of peace, standing armies without the consent of our legislature.

He has affected to render the military independent of and superior to civil power.

He has combined with others to subject us to a jurisdiction foreign to our constitution, and unacknowledged by our laws; giving his assent to their acts of pretended legislation:

For quartering large bodies of armed troops among us:

For protecting them, by mock trial, from punishment for any murders which they should commit on the inhabitants of these states:

For cutting off our trade with all parts of the world:

For imposing taxes on us without our consent:

For depriving us in many cases, of the benefits of trial by jury:

For transporting us beyond seas to be tried for pretended offenses:

For abolishing the free system of English laws in a neighboring province, establishing therein an arbitrary government, and enlarging its boundaries so as to render it at once an example and fit instrument for introducing the same absolute rule in these colonies:

For taking away our charters, abolishing our most valuable laws, and altering fundamentally the forms of our governments:

For suspending our own legislatures, and declaring themselves invested with power to legislate for us in all cases whatsoever.

He has abdicated government here, by declaring us out of his protection and waging war against us.

He has plundered our seas, ravaged our coasts, burned our towns, and destroyed the lives of our people.

He is at this time transporting large armies of foreign mercenaries to complete the works of death, desolation and tyranny, already begun with circumstances of cruelty and perfidy scarcely paralleled in the most barbarous ages, and totally unworthy the head of a civilized nation.

He has constrained our fellow citizens taken captive on the high seas to bear arms against their country, to become the executioners of their friends and brethren, or to fall themselves by their hands.

He has excited domestic insurrections amongst us, and has endeavored to bring on the inhabitants of our frontiers, the merciless Indian savages, whose known rule of warfare, is undistinguished destruction of all ages, sexes and conditions.

In every stage of these oppressions we have petitioned for redress in the most humble terms: our repeated petitions have been answered only by repeated injury. A prince, whose character is thus marked by every act which may define a tyrant, is unfit to be the ruler of a free people.

Nor have we been wanting in attention to our British brethren. We have warned them from time to time of attempts by their legislature to extend an unwarrantable jurisdiction over us. We have reminded them of the circumstances of our emigration and settlement here. We have appealed to their native justice and magnanimity, and we have conjured them by the ties of our common kindred to disavow these usurpations, which would inevitably interrupt our connections and correspondence. They too have been deaf to the voice of justice and of consanguinity. We must, therefore, acquiesce in the necessity, which denounces our separation, and hold them, as we hold the rest of mankind, enemies in war, in peace friends.

We, therefore, the representatives of the United States of America, in General Congress, assembled, appealing to the Supreme Judge of the world for the rectitude of our intentions, do, in the name, and by the authority of the good people of these colonies, solemnly publish and declare, that these united colonies are, and of right ought to be free and independent states; that they are absolved from all allegiance to the British Crown, and that all political connection between them and the state of Great Britain, is and ought to be totally dissolved; and that as free and independent states, they have full power to levy war, conclude peace, contract alliances, establish commerce, and to do all other acts and things which independent states may of right do. And for the support of this declaration, with a firm reliance on the protection of Divine Providence, we mutually pledge to each other our lives, our fortunes and our sacred honor.

New Hampshire: Josiah Bartlett, William Whipple, Matthew Thornton
Massachusetts: John Hancock, Samual Adams, John Adams, Robert Treat Paine, Elbridge Gerry
Rhode Island: Stephen Hopkins, William Ellery
Connecticut: Roger Sherman, Samuel Huntington, William Williams, Oliver Wolcott
New York: William Floyd, Philip Livingston, Francis Lewis, Lewis Morris
New Jersey: Richard Stockton, John Witherspoon, Francis Hopkinson, John Hart, Abraham Clark
Pennsylvania: Robert Morris, Benjamin Rush, Benjamin Franklin, John Morton, George Clymer, James Smith, George Taylor, James Wilson, George Ross
Delaware: Caesar Rodney, George Read, Thomas McKean
Maryland: Samuel Chase, William Paca, Thomas Stone, Charles Carroll of Carrollton
Virginia: George Wythe, Richard Henry Lee, Thomas Jefferson, Benjamin Harrison, Thomas Nelson, Jr., Francis Lightfoot Lee, Carter Braxton
North Carolina: William Hooper, Joseph Hewes, John Penn
South Carolina: Edward Rutledge, Thomas Heyward, Jr., Thomas Lynch, Jr., Arthur Middleton
Georgia: Button Gwinnett, Lyman Hall, George Walton

Source: The Pennsylvania Packet, July 8, 1776

The Constitution of the United States

Here is the complete text of the U.S. Constitution.
The original spelling and capitalization have been retained

We the People of the United States, in Order to form a more perfect Union, establish Justice, insure domestic Tranquility, provide for the common defense, promote the general Welfare, and secure the Blessings of Liberty to ourselves and our Posterity, do ordain and establish this Constitution for the United States of America.

Article I

Section 1. All legislative Powers herein granted shall be vested in a Congress of the United States, which shall consist of a Senate and House of Representatives.

Section 2. The House of Representatives shall be composed of Members chosen every second Year by the People of the several States, and the Electors in each State shall have the Qualifications requisite for Electors of the most numerous Branch of the State Legislature.

No Person shall be a Representative who shall not have attained to the age of twenty five Years, and been seven Years a Citizen of the United States, and who shall not, when elected, be an Inhabitant of that State in which he shall be chosen.

Representatives and direct Taxes shall be apportioned among the several States which may be included within this Union, according to their respective Numbers, which shall be determined by adding to the whole Number of free Persons, including those bound to Service for a Term of Years, and excluding Indians not taxed, three fifths of all other Persons. The actual Enumeration shall be made within three Years after the first Meeting of the Congress of the United States, and within every subsequent Term of ten Years, in such Manner as they shall by Law direct. The Number of Representatives shall not exceed one for every thirty Thousand, but each State shall have at Least one Representative; and until such enumeration shall be made, the State of New Hampshire shall be entitled to chuse three, Massachusetts eight, Rhode-Island and Providence Plantations one, Connecticut five, New-York six, New Jersey four, Pennsylvania eight, Delaware one, Maryland six, Virginia ten, North Carolina five, South Carolina five, and Georgia three.

When vacancies happen in the Representation from any State, the Executive Authority thereof shall issue Writs of Election to fill such Vacancies.

The House of Representatives shall chuse their Speaker and other Officers; and shall have the sole Power of Impeachment.

Section 3. The Senate of the United States shall be composed of two Senators from each State, chosen by the Legislature thereof, for six Years; and each Senator shall have one Vote.

Immediately after they shall be assembled in Consequence of the first Election, they shall be divided as equally as may be into three Classes. The Seats of the Senators of the first Class shall be vacated at the Expiration of the second Year, of the second Class at the Expiration of the fourth Year, and the third Class at the Expiration of the sixth Year, so that one third may be chosen every second Year; and if Vacancies happen by Resignation, or otherwise, during the Recess of the Legislature of any State, the Executive thereof may make temporary Appointments until the next Meeting of the Legislature, which shall then fill such Vacancies.

No Person shall be a Senator who shall not have attained to the Age of thirty Years, and been nine Years a Citizen of the United States and who shall not, when elected, be an Inhabitant of that State for which he shall be chosen.

The Vice President of the United States shall be president of the Senate, but shall have no Vote, unless they be equally divided.

The Senate shall chuse their other Officers, and also a president pro tempore, in the Absence of the Vice President, or when he shall exercise the Office of president of the United States.

The Senate shall have the sole Power to try all Impeachments. When sitting for that Purpose, they shall be on Oath or Affirmation. When the president of the United States is tried, the Chief Justice shall preside: And no Person shall be convicted without the Concurrence of two thirds of the Members present.

Judgment in Cases of Impeachment shall not extend further than to removal from Office, and disqualification to hold and enjoy any Office of Honor, Trust or Profit under the United States:

but the Party convicted shall nevertheless be liable and subject to Indictment, Trial, Judgment and Punishment, according to Law.

Section 4. The Times, Places and Manner of holding Elections for Senators and Representatives, shall be prescribed in each State by the Legislature thereof; but the Congress may at any time by Law make or alter such Regulations, except as to the Places of chusing Senators.

The Congress shall assemble at least once in every Year, and such Meeting shall be on the first Monday in December, unless they shall by Law appoint a different Day.

Section 5. Each House shall be the Judge of the Elections, Returns and Qualifications of its own Members, and a Majority of each shall constitute a Quorum to do Business; but a smaller Number may adjourn from day to day, and may be authorized to compel the Attendance of absent Members, in such Manner, and under such Penalties as each House may provide.

Each House may determine the Rules of its Proceedings, punish its Members for disorderly Behaviour, and, with the Concurrence of two thirds, expel a Member.

Each House shall keep a Journal of its Proceedings, and from time to time publish the same, excepting such Parts as may in their Judgment require Secrecy; and the Yeas and Nays of the Members of either House on any question shall, at the Desire of one fifth of those Present, be entered on the Journal.

Neither House, during the Session of Congress, shall, without the Consent of the other, adjourn for more than three days, nor to any other Place than that in which the two Houses shall be sitting.

Section 6. The Senators and Representatives shall receive a Compensation for their Services, to be ascertained by Law, and paid out of the Treasury of the United States. They shall in all Cases, except Treason, Felony and Breach of the Peace, be privileged from Arrest during their Attendance at the Session of their respective Houses, and in going to and returning from the same; and for any Speech or Debate in either House, they shall not be questioned in any other Place.

No Senator or Representative shall, during the Time for which he was elected, be appointed to any civil Office under the Authority of the United States, which shall have been created, or the Emoluments whereof shall have been increased during such time: and no Person holding any Office under the United States, shall be a Member of either House during his Continuance in Office.

Section 7. All Bills for raising Revenue shall originate in the House of Representatives; but the Senate may propose or concur with Amendments as on other Bills.

Every Bill which shall have passed the House of Representatives and the Senate, shall, before it become a Law, be presented to the president of the United States; if he approve he shall sign it, but if not he shall return it, with his Objections to that House in which it shall have originated, who shall enter the Objections at large on their Journal, and proceed to reconsider it. If after such Reconsideration two thirds of that House shall agree to pass the Bill, it shall be sent, together with the Objections, to the other House, by which it shall likewise be reconsidered, and if approved by two thirds of that House, it shall become a Law. But in all such Cases the Votes of both Houses shall be determined by Yeas and Nays, and the Names of the Persons voting for and against the Bill shall be entered on the Journal of each House respectively. If any Bill shall not be returned by the president within ten Days (Sundays excepted) after it shall have been presented to him, the Same shall be a Law, in like Manner as if he had signed it, unless the Congress by their Adjournment prevent its Return, in which Case it shall not be a Law.

Every Order, Resolution, or Vote to which the Concurrence of the Senate and House of Representatives may be necessary (except on a question of Adjournment) shall be presented to the president of the United States; and before the Same shall take Effect, shall be approved by him, or being disapproved by him, shall be repassed by two thirds of the Senate and House of Representatives, according to the Rules and Limitations prescribed in the Case of a Bill.

Section 8. The Congress shall have Power To lay and collect Taxes, Duties, Imposts and Excises, to pay the Debts and provide for the common Defense and general Welfare of the United States; but all Duties, Imposts and Excises shall be uniform throughout the United States;

To borrow Money on the credit of the United States;

To regulate Commerce with foreign Nations, and among the several States, and with the Indian Tribes;

To establish an uniform Rule of Naturalization, and uniform Laws on the subject of Bankruptcies throughout the United States;

To coin Money, regulate the Value thereof, and of foreign Coin, and fix the Standard of Weights and Measures;

To provide for the Punishment of counterfeiting the Securities and current Coin of the United States;

To establish Post Offices and post Roads;

To promote the Progress of Science and useful Arts, by securing for limited Times to Authors and Inventors the exclusive Right to their respective Writings and Discoveries;

To constitute Tribunals inferior to the Supreme Court;

To define and punish Piracies and Felonies committed on the high Seas, and Offences against the Law of Nations;

To declare War, grant Letters of Marque and Reprisal, and make Rules concerning Captures on Land and Water;

To raise and support Armies, but no Appropriation of Money to that Use shall be for a longer Term than two Years;

To provide and maintain a Navy;

To make Rules for the Government and Regulation of the land and naval Forces;

To provide for calling forth the Militia to execute the Laws of the Union, suppress Insurrections and repel Invasions;

To provide for organizing, arming, and disciplining, the Militia, and for governing such Part of them as may be employed in the Service of the United States, reserving to the States respectively, the Appointment of the Officers, and the Authority of training the Militia according to the discipline prescribed by Congress;

To exercise exclusive Legislation in all Cases whatsoever, over such District (not exceeding ten Miles square) as may, by Cession of particular States, and the Acceptance of Congress, become the Seat of the Government of the United States, and to exercise like Authority over all Places purchased by the Consent of the Legislature of the State in which the Same shall be, for the Erection of Forts, Magazines, Arsenals, dock-Yards, and other needful Buildings;--And

To make all Laws which shall be necessary and proper for carrying into Execution the foregoing Powers, and all other Powers vested by this Constitution in the Government of the United States, or in any Department or Officer thereof.

Section 9. The Migration or Importation of such Persons as any of the States now existing shall think proper to admit, shall not be prohibited by the Congress prior to the Year one thousand eight hundred and eight, but a Tax or duty may be imposed on such Importation, not exceeding ten dollars for each Person.

The Privilege of the Writ of Habeas Corpus shall not be suspended, unless when in Cases of Rebellion or Invasion the public Safety may require it.

No Bill of Attainder or ex post facto Law shall be passed.

No Capitation, or other direct, Tax shall be laid, unless in Proportion to the Census or Enumeration herein before directed to be taken.

No Tax or Duty shall be laid on Articles exported from any State.

No Preference shall be given by any Regulation of Commerce or Revenue to the Ports of one State over those of another: nor shall Vessels bound to, or from, one State, be obliged to enter, clear or pay Duties in another.

No Money shall be drawn from the Treasury, but in Consequence of Appropriations made by Law; and a regular Statement and Account of Receipts and Expenditures of all public Money shall be published from time to time.

No Title of Nobility shall be granted by the United States: And no Person holding any Office of Profit or Trust under them, shall, without the Consent of the Congress, accept of any present, Emolument, Office, or Title, of any kind whatever, from any King, Prince, or foreign State.

Section 10. No State shall enter into any Treaty, Alliance, or Confederation; grant Letters of Marque and Reprisal; coin Money; emit Bills of Credit; make any Thing but gold and silver Coin a Tender in Payment of Debts; pass any Bill of Attainder, ex post facto Law, or Law impairing the Obligation of Contracts, or grant any Title of Nobility.

No State shall, without the Consent of the Congress, lay any Imposts or Duties on Imports or Exports, except what may be absolutely necessary for executing its inspection Laws: and the net Produce of all Duties and Imposts, laid by any State on Imports or Exports, shall be for the Use of the Treasury of the United States; and all such Laws shall be subject to the Revision and Control of the Congress.

No State shall, without the Consent of Congress, lay any Duty of Tonnage, keep Troops, or Ships of War in time of Peace, enter into any Agreement or Compact with another State, or with a foreign Power, or engage in War, unless actually invaded, or in such imminent Danger as will not admit of delay.

Article II

Section 1. The executive Power shall be vested in a president of the United States of America. He shall hold his Office during the Term of four Years, and, together with the Vice President, chosen for the same Term, be elected, as follows:

Each State shall appoint, in such Manner as the Legislature thereof may direct, a Number of Electors, equal to the whole Number of Senators and Representatives to which the State may be entitled in the Congress: but no Senator or Representative, or Person holding an Office of Trust or Profit under the United States, shall be appointed an Elector.

The Electors shall meet in their respective States, and vote by Ballot for two Persons, of whom one at least shall not be an Inhabitant of the same State with themselves. And they shall make a List of all the Persons voted for, and of the Number of Votes for each; which List they shall sign and certify, and transmit sealed to the Seat of the Government of the United States, directed to the president of the Senate. The president of the Senate shall, in the Presence of the Senate and House of Representatives, open all the Certificates, and the Votes shall then be counted. The Person having the greatest Number of Votes shall be the president, if such Number be a Majority of the whole Number of Electors appointed; and if there be more than one who have such Majority, and have an equal Number of Votes, then the House of Representatives shall immediately chuse by Ballot one of them for president; and if no Person have a Majority, then from the five highest on the List the said House shall in like Manner chuse the President. But in chusing the President, the Votes shall be taken by States, the Representation from each State having one Vote; A quorum for this Purpose shall consist of a Member or Members from two thirds of the States, and a Majority of all the States shall be necessary to a Choice. In every Case, after the Choice of the President, the Person having the greatest Number of Votes of the Electors shall be the Vice President. But if there should remain two or more who have equal Votes, the Senate shall chuse from them by Ballot the Vice President.

The Congress may determine the Time of chusing the Electors, and the Day on which they shall give their Votes; which Day shall be the same throughout the United States.

No Person except a natural born Citizen, or a Citizen of the United States, at the time of the Adoption of this Constitution, shall be eligible to the Office of President; neither shall any Person be eligible to that Office who shall not have attained to the Age of thirty five Years, and been fourteen Years a Resident within the United States.

In Case of the Removal of the President from Office, or of his Death, Resignation, or Inability to discharge the Powers and Duties of the said Office, the Same shall devolve on the Vice President, and the Congress may by Law provide for the Case of Removal, Death, Resignation or Inability, both of the President and Vice President, declaring what Officer shall then act as President, and such Officer shall act accordingly, until the Disability be removed, or a President shall be elected.

The President shall, at stated Times, receive for his Services, a Compensation, which shall neither be encreased nor diminished during the Period for which he shall have been elected, and he shall not receive within that Period any other Emolument from the United States, or any of them.

Before he enter on the Execution of his Office, he shall take the following Oath or Affirmation:--"I do solemnly swear (or affirm) that I will faithfully execute the Office of President of the United States, and will to the best of my Ability, preserve, protect and defend the Constitution of the United States."

Section 2. The President shall be Commander in Chief of the Army and Navy of the United States, and of the Militia of the several States, when called into the actual Service of the United States; he may require the Opinion, in writing, of the principal Officer in each of the executive Departments, upon any Subject relating to the Duties of their respective Offices, and he shall have Power to grant Reprieves and Pardons for Offences against the United States, except in Cases of Impeachment.

He shall have Power, by and with the Advice and Consent of the Senate, to make Treaties, provided two thirds of the Senators present concur; and he shall nominate, and by and with the Advice and Consent of the Senate, shall appoint Ambassadors, other public Ministers and Consuls, Judges of the supreme Court, and all other Officers of the United States, whose Appointments are not herein otherwise provided for, and which shall be established by Law: but the Congress may by Law vest the Appointment of such inferior Officers, as they think proper, in the President alone, in the Courts of Law, or in the Heads of Departments.

The President shall have Power to fill up all Vacancies that may happen during the Recess of the Senate, by granting Commissions which shall expire at the End of their next Session.

Section 3. He shall from time to time give to the Congress Information of the State of the Union, and recommend to their Consideration such Measures as he shall judge necessary and expedient; he may, on extraordinary Occasions, convene both Houses, or either of them, and in Case of Disagreement between them, with Respect to the Time of Adjournment, he may adjourn them to such Time as he shall think proper; he shall receive Ambassadors and other public Ministers; he shall take Care that the Laws be faithfully executed, and shall Commission all the Officers of the United States.

Section 4. The President, Vice President and all civil Officers of the United States, shall be removed from Office on Impeachment for, and Conviction of, Treason, Bribery, or other high Crimes and Misdemeanors.

Article III

Section 1. The judicial Power of the United States, shall be vested in one supreme Court, and in such inferior Courts as the Congress may from time to time ordain and establish. The Judges, both of the supreme and inferior Courts, shall hold their Offices during good Behavior, and shall, at stated Times, receive for their Services, a Compensation, which shall not be diminished during their Continuance in Office.

Section 2. The judicial Power shall extend to all Cases, in Law and Equity, arising under this Constitution, the Laws of the United States, and Treaties made, or which shall be made, under their Authority;--to all Cases affecting Ambassadors, other public Ministers and Consuls;--to all Cases of admiralty and maritime Jurisdiction;--to Controversies to which the United States shall be a Party;--to Controversies between two or more States;--between a State and Citizens of another State;--between Citizens of different States;--between Citizens of the same State claiming Lands under Grants of different States, and between a State, or the Citizens thereof, and foreign States, Citizens or Subjects.

In all Cases affecting Ambassadors, other public Ministers and Consuls, and those in which a State shall be Party, the Supreme Court shall have original Jurisdiction. In all the other Cases before mentioned, the Supreme Court shall have appellate Jurisdiction, both as to Law and Fact, with such Exceptions, and under such Regulations as the Congress shall make.

The Trial of all Crimes, except in Cases of Impeachment, shall be by Jury; and such Trial shall be held in the State where the said Crimes shall have been committed; but when not committed within any State, the Trial shall be at such Place or Places as the Congress may by Law have directed.

Section 3. Treason against the United States, shall consist only in levying War against them, or in adhering to their Enemies, giving them Aid and Comfort. No Person shall be convicted of Treason unless on the Testimony of two Witnesses to the same overt Act, or on Confession in open Court.

The Congress shall have Power to declare the Punishment of Treason, but no Attainder of Treason shall work Corruption of Blood, or Forfeiture except during the Life of the Person attainted.

Article IV

Section 1. Full Faith and Credit shall be given in each State to the public Acts, Records, and judicial Proceedings of every other State. And the Congress may by general Laws prescribe the Manner in which such Acts, Records, and Proceedings shall be proved, and the Effect thereof.

Section 2. The Citizens of each State shall be entitled to all Privileges and Immunities of Citizens in the several States.

A Person charged in any State with Treason, Felony, or other Crime, who shall flee from Justice, and be found in another State, shall on Demand of the executive Authority of the State from which he fled, be delivered up, to be removed to the State having Jurisdiction of the Crime.

No Person held to Service or Labor in one State, under the Laws thereof, escaping into another, shall, in Consequence of any Law or Regulation therein, be discharged from such Service or Labor, but shall be delivered up on Claim of the Party to whom such Service or Labor may be due.

Section 3. New States may be admitted by the Congress into this Union; but no new States shall be formed or erected within the Jurisdiction of any other State; nor any State be formed by the Junction of two or more States, or Parts of States, without the Consent of the Legislatures of the States concerned as well as of the Congress.

The Congress shall have Power to dispose of and make all needful Rules and Regulations respecting the Territory or other Property belonging to the United States; and nothing in this Constitution shall be so construed as to Prejudice any Claims of the United States, or of any particular State.

Section 4. The United States shall guarantee to every State in this Union a Republican Form of Government, and shall protect each of them against Invasion; and on Application of the Legislature, or of the Executive (when the Legislature cannot be convened) against domestic Violence.

Article V

The Congress, whenever two thirds of both Houses shall deem it necessary, shall propose Amendments to this Constitution, or, on the Application of the Legislatures of two thirds of the several States, shall call a Convention for proposing Amendments, which, in either Case, shall be valid to all Intents and Purposes, as Part of this Constitution, when ratified by the Legislatures of three fourths of the several States, or by Conventions in three fourths thereof, as the one or the other Mode of Ratification may be proposed by the Congress; Provided that no Amendment which may be made prior to the Year One thousand eight hundred and eight shall in any Manner affect the first and fourth Clauses in the Ninth Section of the first Article; and that no State, without its Consent, shall be deprived of its equal Suffrage in the Senate.

Article VI

All Debts contracted and Engagements entered into, before the Adoption of this Constitution, shall be as valid against the United States under this Constitution, as under the Confederation.

This Constitution, and the Laws of the United States which shall be made in Pursuance thereof; and all Treaties made, or which shall be made, under the Authority of the United States, shall be the supreme Law of the Land; and the Judges in every State shall be bound thereby, any Thing in the Constitution or Laws of any State to the Contrary not with-standing.

The Senators and Representatives before mentioned, and the Members of the several State Legislatures, and all executive and judicial Officers, both of the United States and of the several States, shall be bound by Oath or Affirmation, to support this Constitution; but no religious Test shall ever be required as a Qualification to any Office or public Trust under the United States.

Article VII

The Ratification of the Conventions of nine States, shall be sufficient for the Establishment of this Constitution between the States so ratifying the Same.

Done in Convention by the Unanimous Consent of the States present the Seventeenth Day of September in the Year of our Lord one thousand seven hundred and Eighty seven and of the Independence of the United States of America the Twelfth

In witness whereof We have hereunto subscribed our Names,

George Washington--President and deputy from Virginia

New Hampshire: John Langdon, Nicholas Gilman

Massachusetts: Nathaniel Gorham, Rufus King

Connecticut: William Samuel Johnson, Roger Sherman

New York: Alexander Hamilton

New Jersey: William Livingston, David Brearly, William Paterson, Jonathan Dayton

Pennsylvania: Benjamin Franklin, Thomas Mifflin, Robert Morris, George Clymer, Thomas FitzSimons, Jared Ingersoll, James Wilson, Governor Morris

Delaware: George Read, Gunning Bedford, Jr., John Dickinson, Richard Bassett, Jacob Broom

Maryland: James McHenry, Daniel of Saint Thomas Jenifer, Daniel Carroll

Virginia: John Blair, James Madison, Jr.

North Carolina: William Blount, Richard Dobbs Spaight, Hugh Williamson

South Carolina: John Rutledge, Charles Cotesworth Pinckney, Charles Pinckney, Pierce Butler

Georgia: William Few, Abraham Baldwin

Source: *The Pennsylvania Packet*, September 19, 1787

AMENDMENTS TO THE U.S. CONSTITUTION

*The first Ten Amendments to the United States Constitution are the **Bill of Rights**. The Bill of Rights was ratified as part of a gentlemen's agreement among our Founding Fathers. There was resistance to the approval of the United States Constitution by Thomas Jefferson and others because too much power was given to the Federal government, and American citizens were unprotected. The Constitution was ratified in 1788, and the Federalists kept their word and ratified the Bill of Rights in 1791 to protect the individual rights of American citizens.*

The Bill of Rights

- First Amendment – Establishment Clause, Free Exercise Clause; freedom of speech, of the press, Freedom of Religion, and of assembly; right to petition.
  Congress shall make no law respecting an establishment of religion, or prohibiting the free exercise thereof; or abridging the freedom of speech, or of the press; or the right of the people peaceably to assemble, and to petition the Government for a redress of grievances.

- <u>Second Amendment</u> – <u>Militia (United States)</u>, <u>Sovereign state</u>, <u>Right to keep and bear arms</u>.
  A well-regulated Militia, being necessary to the security of a free State, the right of the people to keep and bear Arms, shall not be infringed. [5][6]

- <u>Third Amendment</u> – Protection from <u>quartering</u> of troops.
  No Soldier shall, in time of peace be quartered in any house, without the consent of the Owner, nor in time of war, but in a manner to be prescribed by law.

- <u>Fourth Amendment</u> – Protection from unreasonable <u>search and seizure</u>.
  The right of the people to be secure in their persons, houses, papers, and effects, against unreasonable searches and seizures, shall not be violated, and no <u>Warrants</u> shall issue, but upon probable cause, supported by Oath or affirmation, and particularly describing the place to be searched, and the persons or things to be seized.

- <u>Fifth Amendment</u> – <u>due process</u>, <u>double jeopardy</u>, <u>self-incrimination</u>, <u>eminent domain</u>.
  No person shall be held to answer for any capital, or otherwise infamous crime, unless on a presentment or indictment of a Grand Jury, except in cases arising in the land or naval forces, or in the Militia, when in actual service in time of War or public danger; nor shall any person be subject for the same offence to be twice put in jeopardy of life or limb; nor shall be compelled in any criminal case to be a witness against himself, nor be deprived of life, liberty, or property, without due process of law; nor shall private property be taken for public use, without just compensation.

- <u>Sixth Amendment</u> – <u>Trial by jury</u> and <u>rights of the accused</u>; <u>Confrontation Clause</u>, <u>speedy trial</u>, <u>public trial</u>, <u>right to counsel</u>.
  In all criminal prosecutions, the accused shall enjoy the right to a speedy and public trial, by an impartial jury of the State and district where in the crime shall have been committed, which district shall have been previously ascertained by law, and to be informed of the nature and cause of the accusation; to be confronted with the witnesses against him; to have compulsory process for obtaining witnesses in his favor, and to have the Assistance of Counsel for his defense.

- Seventh Amendment – <u>Civil</u> trial by jury.
  In suits at common law, where the value in controversy shall exceed twenty dollars, the right of trial by jury shall be preserved, and no fact tried by a jury, shall be otherwise re-examined in any court of the United States, than according to the rules of the common law.

- Eighth Amendment – Prohibition of <u>excessive bail</u> and <u>cruel and unusual punishment</u>.
  Excessive bail shall not be required, nor excessive fines imposed, nor cruel and unusual punishments inflicted.

- Ninth Amendment – Protection of rights not specifically enumerated in the Bill of Rights.
  The enumeration in the Constitution, of certain rights, shall not be construed to deny or disparage others retained by the people.

- Tenth Amendment – Powers of States and people.
  The powers not delegated to the United States by the Constitution, nor prohibited by it to the States, are reserved to the States respectively, or to the people.

AMENDMENTS 11–27 TO THE CONSTITUTION OF THE UNITED STATES

*This list includes **Amendments 11 to 27**, and provides a brief historical background on the reason for its inclusion as an Amendment to the United States Constitution.*

THE ELEVENTH AMENDMENT

This amendment arose from states' rights, and was designed to keep suits between states and their citizens out of federal courts. Ratification was completed on February 7, 1795.

The Judicial power of the United States shall not be construed to extend to any suit in law or equity, commenced or prosecuted against one of the United States by Citizens of another State, or by Citizens or Subjects of any Foreign State.

THE TWELFTH AMENDMENT

The Twelfth Amendment requires separate balloting in the Electoral College for President and Vice President, to avoid the difficulties encountered when the 1804 election was thrown into the House of Representatives. It took 36 ballots before Thomas Jefferson was chosen as the third president of the United States! Ratification was completed on June 15, 1804.

The Electors shall meet in their respective states, and vote by ballot for President and Vice President, one of whom, at least, shall not be an inhabitant of the same state with themselves; they shall name in their ballots the person voted for as President, and in distinct ballots the person voted for as Vice President, and they shall make distinct lists of all persons voted for as President, and of all persons voted for as Vice President, and of the number of votes for each, which lists they shall sign and certify, and transmit sealed to the seat of the government of the United States, directed to the President of the Senate;--The President of the Senate shall, in the presence of the Senate and House of Representatives, open all the certificates and the votes shall then be counted;--The person having the greatest number of votes for President, shall be the President, if such number be a majority of the whole number of Electors appointed; and if no person have such majority, then from the persons having the highest numbers not exceeding three on the list of those voted for as President, the House of Representatives shall choose immediately, by ballot, the President. But in choosing the President, the votes shall be taken by states, the representation from each state having one vote; a quorum for this purpose shall consist of a member or members from two-thirds of the states, and a majority of all the states shall be necessary to a choice. And if the House of Representatives shall not choose a President whenever the right of choice shall devolve upon them, before the fourth day of March next following, then the Vice President shall act as President, as in the case of the death or other constitutional disability of the President. The person having the greatest number of votes as Vice President, shall be the Vice President, if such number be a majority of the whole number of Electors appointed, and if no person have a majority, then from the two highest numbers on the list, the Senate shall choose the Vice President; a quorum for the purpose shall consist of two-thirds of the whole number of Senators, and a majority of the whole number shall be necessary to a choice. But no person constitutionally ineligible to the office of President shall be eligible to that of Vice President of the United States.

THE THIRTEENTH AMENDMENT

The Thirteenth Amendment followed the Civil War and put an end to African-American slavery. Ratification was completed on December 6, 1865.

Section 1. Neither slavery nor involuntary servitude, except as a punishment for crime whereof the party shall have been duly convicted, shall exist within the United States, or any place subject to their jurisdiction.

Section 2. Congress shall have power to enforce this article by appropriate legislation.

THE FOURTEENTH AMENDMENT

The Fourteenth Amendment was the second of three amendments following the Civil War. This amendment defined American citizenship, but also placed restrictions on former Confederates. This amendment is often quoted by the Supreme Court as providing "equal protection" to all citizens and was referenced in the 2000 Florida recount decision. Ratification was completed on July 9, 1868.

Section 1. All persons born or naturalized in the United States, and subject to the jurisdiction thereof, are citizens of the United States and of the State wherein they reside. No State shall make or enforce any law which shall abridge the privileges or immunities of citizens of the United States; nor shall any State deprive any person of life, liberty, or property, without due process of law; nor deny to any person within its jurisdiction the equal protection of the laws.

Section 2. Representatives shall be apportioned among the several States according to their respective numbers, counting the whole number of persons in each State, excluding Indians not taxed. But when the right to vote at any election for the choice of electors for President and Vice President of the United States, Representatives in Congress, the Executive and Judicial officers of a State, or the members of the Legislature thereof, is denied to any of the male inhabitants of such State, being twenty-one years of age and citizens of the United States, or in any way abridged, except for participation in rebellion, or other crime, the basis of representation therein shall be reduced in the proportion which the number of such male citizens shall bear to the whole number of male citizens twenty-one years of age in such State.

Section 3. No person shall be a Senator or Representative in Congress, or elector of President and Vice President, or hold any office, civil or military, under the United States, or under any

State, who, having previously taken an oath, as a member of Congress, or as an officer of the United States, or as a member of any State legislature, or as an executive or judicial officer of any State, to support the Constitution of the United States, shall have engaged in insurrection or rebellion against the same, or given aid or comfort to the enemies thereof. But Congress may by a vote of two-thirds of each House, remove such disability.

Section 4. The validity of the public debt of the United States, authorized by law, including debts incurred for payment of pensions and bounties for services in suppressing insurrection or rebellion, shall not be questioned. But neither the United States nor any State shall assume or pay any debt or obligation incurred in aid of insurrection or rebellion against the United States, or any claim for the loss or emancipation of any slave; but all such debts, obligations and claims shall be held illegal and void.

Section 5. The Congress shall have power to enforce, by appropriate legislation, the provisions of this article.

THE FIFTEENTH AMENDMENT
The Fifteenth Amendment was the third amendment following the Civil War that addressed the issue of African-American slavery. This amendment prohibited states from denying the right to vote because of a person's race or because a person had been a slave. Even with the ratification of this amendment, Indians and women were still not yet allowed to vote! The amendment was ratified in February of 1870.

Section 1. The right of citizens of the United States to vote shall not be denied or abridged by the United States or by any State on account of race, color, or previous condition of servitude.

Section 2. The Congress shall have power to enforce this article by appropriate legislation.

THE SIXTEENTH AMENDMENT
The Sixteenth Amendment began the federal income tax! Ratification was completed on February 3, 1913.

The Congress shall have power to lay and collect taxes on incomes, from whatever source derived, without apportionment among the several States, and without regard to any census or enumeration.

THE SEVENTEENTH AMENDMENT

The Seventeenth Amendment allowed election of Senators directly by popular vote.
Ratification was completed on April 8, 1913.

The Senate of the United States shall be composed of two Senators from each State, elected by the people thereof, for six years; and each Senator shall have one vote. The electors in each State shall have the qualifications requisite for electors of the most numerous branch of the State legislatures.

When vacancies happen in the representation of any State in the Senate, the executive authority of such State shall issue writs of election to fill such vacancies: Provided, That the legislature of any State may empower the executive thereof to make temporary appointments until the people fill the vacancies by election as the legislature may direct.

This amendment shall not be so construed as to affect the election or term of any Senator chosen before it becomes valid as part of the Constitution.

THE EIGHTEENTH AMENDMENT

The Eighteenth Amendment began the Prohibition of alcohol.
This amendment was ratified in January 1919.

Section 1. After one year from the ratification of this article the manufacture, sale, or transportation of intoxicating liquors within, the importation thereof into, or the exportation thereof from the United States and all territory subject to the jurisdiction thereof for beverage purposes is hereby prohibited.

Section 2. The Congress and the several States shall have concurrent power to enforce this article by appropriate legislation.

Section 3. This article shall be inoperative unless it shall have been ratified as an amendment to the Constitution by the legislatures of the several States, as provided in the Constitution, within seven years from the date of the submission hereof to the States by the Congress.

THE NINETEENTH AMENDMENT

The Nineteenth Amendment granted women suffrage or the right to vote.
This amendment was ratified by August of 1920.

The right of citizens of the United States to vote shall not be denied or abridged by the United States or by any State on account of sex.

Congress shall have power to enforce this article by appropriate legislation.

THE TWENTIETH AMENDMENT

The Twentieth Amendment, commonly called the "Lame Duck Amendment," shortened the period between Election Day and Inauguration Day from March 4 to January 20 for the president, and to January 3 for the opening session for Congress. This was ratified February 6, 1933.

Section 1. The terms of the President and Vice President shall end at noon on the 20th day of January, and the terms of Senators and Representatives at noon on the 3d day of January, of the years in which such terms would have ended if this article had not been ratified; and the terms of their successors shall then begin.

Section 2. The Congress shall assemble at least once in every year, and such meeting shall begin at noon on the 3d day of January, unless they shall by law appoint a different day.

Section 3. If, at the time fixed for the beginning of the term of the President, the President-elect shall have died, the Vice President-elect shall become President. If a President shall not have been chosen before the time fixed for the beginning of his term, or if the President-elect shall have failed to qualify, then the Vice President-elect shall act as President until a President shall have qualified; and the Congress may by law provide for the case wherein neither a President-elect nor a Vice President-elect shall have qualified, declaring who shall then act as President, or the manner in which one who is to act shall be selected, and such person shall act accordingly until a President or Vice President shall have qualified.

Section 4. The Congress may by law provide for the case of the death of any of the persons from whom the House of Representatives may choose a President whenever the right of choice shall have devolved upon them, and for the case of the death of any of the persons from whom the Senate may choose a Vice President whenever the right of choice shall have devolved upon them.

Section 5. Sections 1 and 2 shall take effect on the 15th day of October following the ratification of this article.

Section 6. This article shall be inoperative unless it shall have been ratified as an amendment to the Constitution by the legislatures of three-fourths of the several States within seven years from the date of its submission.

THE TWENTY-FIRST AMENDMENT

This amendment repealed Prohibition and was ratified on December 5, 1933.

Section 1. The eighteenth article of amendment to the Constitution of the United States is hereby repealed.

Section 2. The transportation or importation into any State, Territory, or possession of the United States for delivery or use therein of intoxicating liquors, in violation of the laws thereof, is hereby prohibited.

Section 3. This article shall be inoperative unless it shall have been ratified as an amendment to the Constitution by conventions in the several States, as provided in the Constitution, within seven years from the date of the submission hereof to the States by the Congress.

THE TWENTY-SECOND AMENDMENT

This amendment began the two-term limit of the U.S.
president and was ratified February 27, 1951.

Section 1. No person shall be elected to the office of the President more than twice, and no person who has held the office of President, or acted as President, for more than two years of a term to which some other person was elected President shall be elected to the office of the President more than once. But this article shall not apply to any person holding the office of President when this article was proposed by the Congress, and shall not prevent any person who may be holding the office of President, or acting as President, during the term within which this article becomes operative from holding the office of President or acting as President during the remainder of such term.

Section 2. This article shall be inoperative unless it shall have been ratified as an amendment to the Constitution by the legislatures of three-fourths of the several states within seven years from the date of its submission to the states by the Congress.

THE TWENTY-THIRD AMENDMENT
This amendment gave the presidential vote to Washington,
D.C., and was ratified March 29, 1961.

Section 1. The District constituting the seat of government of the United States shall appoint in such manner as the Congress may direct:

A number of electors of President and Vice President equal to the whole number of Senators and Representatives in Congress to which the District would be entitled if it were a state, but in no event more than the least populous state; they shall be in addition to those appointed by the states, but they shall be considered, for the purposes of the election of President and Vice President, to be electors appointed by a state; and they shall meet in the District and perform such duties as provided by the twelfth article of amendment.

Section 2. The Congress shall have power to enforce this article by appropriate legislation.

THE TWENTY-FOURTH AMENDMENT
This amendment nullified the poll tax and was ratified January 23, 1964.

Section 1. The right of citizens of the United States to vote in any primary or other election for President or Vice President, for electors for President or Vice President, or for Senator or Representative in Congress, shall not be denied or abridged by the United States or any state by reason of failure to pay any poll tax or other tax.

Section 2. The Congress shall have power to enforce this article by appropriate legislation.

THE TWENTY-FIFTH AMENDMENT
This amendment has to do with presidential succession and was ratified February 10, 1967.

Section 1. In case of the removal of the President from office or of his death or resignation, the Vice President shall become President.

Section 2. Whenever there is a vacancy in the office of the Vice President, the President shall nominate a Vice President who shall take office upon confirmation by a majority vote of both Houses of Congress.

Section 3. Whenever the President transmits to the President pro tempore of the Senate and the Speaker of the House of Representatives his written declaration that he is unable to discharge the powers and duties of his office, and until he transmits to them a written declaration to the contrary, such powers and duties shall be discharged by the Vice President as Acting President.

Section 4. Whenever the Vice President and a majority of either the principal officers of the executive departments or of such other body as Congress may by law provide, transmit to the President pro tempore of the Senate and the Speaker of the House of Representatives their written declaration that the President is unable to discharge the powers and duties of his office, the Vice President shall immediately assume the powers and duties of the office as Acting President.

Thereafter, when the President transmits to the President pro tempore of the Senate and the Speaker of the House of Representatives his written declaration that no inability exists, he shall resume the powers and duties of his office unless the Vice President and a majority of either the principal officers of the executive department or of such other body as Congress may by law provide, transmit within four days to the President pro tempore of the Senate and the Speaker of the House of Representatives their written declaration that the President is unable to discharge the powers and duties of his office. Thereupon Congress shall decide the issue, assembling within forty-eight hours for that purpose if not in session. If the Congress, within twenty-one days after receipt of the latter written declaration, or, if Congress is not in session, within twenty-one days after Congress is required to assemble, determines by two-thirds vote of both Houses that the President is unable to discharge the powers and duties of his office, the Vice President shall continue to discharge the same as Acting President; otherwise, the President shall resume the powers and duties of his office.

THE TWENTY-SIXTH AMENDMENT
This amendment gave the right to vote to eighteen-year-old citizens and was ratified July 1, 1971.

Section 1. The right of citizens of the United States, who are 18 years of age or older, to vote, shall not be denied or abridged by the United States or any state on account of age.

Section 2. The Congress shall have the power to enforce this article by appropriate legislation.

THE TWENTY-SEVENTH AMENDMENT

This amendment concerned compensation of Members of Congress and was ratified May 7, 1992.

No law varying the compensation for the services of the Senators and Representatives shall take effect until an election of Representatives shall have intervened.

Chapter Six
Defense of the United States
Defense—<u>The</u> Single Most Important
Function of the United States Government

"A veteran—whether active duty, retired, or National Guard or Reserve—is someone who, at one point in his or her life, wrote a blank check made payable to 'The United States of America,' for an amount of 'up to and including my life.' That is honor, and there are way too many people in this country who no longer understand it."
—Author unknown

The Greatest Generation

Of the sixteen million soldiers who served in World War II, there are just one third of them still living today. These folks are dying at the rate of more than 1,100 per day. The average age of those who are still with us is eighty-five. "The Greatest Generation" of Americans seldom spoke of their war years once they returned home in 1945 and 1946. Perhaps these soldiers wanted to forget their experience and get on with their lives, just grateful that they had survived and not wanting to dwell on the friends they had left behind. Or perhaps they just saw their service to their country in the same light that our founding fathers had, which was that it was simply *"their duty"* to serve. It may be different for each of them but what is certainly common among *all* of them is that once they returned home in 1945 and 1946, they were ready to simply get on with their lives and not dwell on the past. I have had the good fortune to know many of these soldiers from "the Greatest Generation," and to a person they each have exemplified the exact same humility and quiet sense of duty to their nation and to their families.

While I was writing this book, I had a long conversation with Russell E. (Eugene) Gilmer, one of the individuals to whom this book is dedicated. Gene (his middle name is Eugene and he prefers to go by Gene) is my stepfather. My own father died when I was four years old, and my mother remarried when I was eleven. Gene saw me through those teenage years, which as everyone knows are not always easy. During my recent conversation with Gene, he shared many of his experiences from World War II. Gene had never shared these stories while we were growing up. We began the conversation with a discussion about this book, for I had sent excerpts from the book to all of my clients in late June of 2009. Gene is very supportive of this work and appreciates that someone is boldly advancing the causes of Liberty and Freedom. Gene explained that it is difficult for him to understand much of what has transpired in our government these past few months, for as he says, ***"It makes no sense."*** Gene often simply turns off the television.

Gene and four of his friends drove to Indianapolis and enlisted into the military shortly after graduating from high school in 1941. This was the course of action most young men took during this time in our history. Gene saw World War II in both the European and Pacific fronts. Gene ended up in the Navy and was one of the crew on a landing craft that shuttled the soldiers back and forth between England and the beaches of Omaha and Utah at Normandy during the D-Day invasion. Gene experienced all-out war right before his eyes for several days as his ship shuttled soldiers from England to France. Once Europe was liberated and Germany defeated, Gene's group was sent to the Pacific via the United States to make ready for an invasion of Japan.

Before arriving safely in port, Gene's ship was caught in a fierce hurricane off the Carolina coast, where they were forced to "ride it out" for several days before coming ashore. Ironically, Gene said the experience with the hurricane could actually compete with some of the worst battles of the war. After a short stay in the United States, Gene's group headed for Japan thru the Panama canal. As it turned out, the atomic bomb ended the war sooner than most thought would be the case; however, that event didn't take Gene out of harm's way. He was among those sent in to clear Tokyo Harbor of mines to make way for the arrival of Douglas MacArthur on the USS Missouri for the signing of the peace treaty with Japan. Gene explained that they first sent in two wooden-hull ships (wooden hulls were used because steel hulls would attract the mines) with a cable stretched between them below the surface to cut loose the mines, allowing them to surface to the top of the water. Once the mines were floating free, the sailors shot them with high-powered 30-30 rifles to detonate the mines. With this task finished, Gene's group sailed home for America via Hawaii. Gene still has a painting of his ship that one of his fellow onboard sailors had painted while they were in port at Honolulu after the war. "Diamond Head" appears in the background of the scene. Gene paid his fellow shipmate $10 for the work.

This book is also dedicated to George Huffman, my business partner of several years in the insurance business. George had already graduated from Purdue University before World War II began. George was in the U.S. Army Artillery and was responsible for an eight-inch howitzer gun. These guns could shoot several miles. George was among those who landed at Normandy and liberated Europe. George once told me a story about the day they went ashore at Normandy. Once the ramp on the ship was dropped, you were ordered to hit the gas at full throttle and remain at full throttle until you were on dry land. Otherwise, the engine might stall or die, leaving **you** "dead in the water." The soldier who was driving the vehicle in which George was a passenger took his foot off the accelerator when the cold water from the Atlantic Ocean "hit him." This could have meant a certain end to the landing for their group. So when the driver pulled his foot back from the gas pedal, George simply took his left foot and, as he described, ***"I mashed down on top of the driver's foot with all my might, and stayed there until we were ashore."***

George's division marched through France, liberated Europe, and then went on to fight in "Hitler's last stand," which was the Battle of the Bulge in Belgium. No one expected Hitler to make this attack, and the entire Allied Army was caught by surprise when it occurred. George explained to me one day that with all military operations, there is a certain order that is strictly adhered to. As an Army advances, the artillery is always shooting in their forward position as they progress. George said that in mid-December of 1944, his group got an order from on high to turn their guns 180 degrees and commence firing. George's commanding officer couldn't believe the order, for normally that would mean firing on your ***own forces*** as they were coming up behind you. When the order was questioned, the reply very quickly came back that, under no un-certain terms, they were to do precisely as ordered. As it turned out, German forces were surrounding the Allies by making a sudden advance on the Allied lines. This created a bulge (thus the name of the battle) in the Allied line, allowing the Germans to be at their rear. The Battle of the Bulge became the single ***biggest and bloodiest*** battle that American forces experienced in World War II (from Wikipedia).

The other two individuals to whom this book is dedicated are J. Ben Good and Gordon Laymon. J. Ben Good served in the Navy in World War II. Ben served on a patrol craft (or PC boat) in the South Pacific. These patrol crafts were used in hunting down Japanese submarines and dropping depth charges. Ben's wife Elizabeth waited patiently at home with their infant son Ted for Ben's return after the war. The Laymon family has been involved in our local telephone company for over three generations. During World War II, there was a desperate need in the military for every skill imaginable. One area requiring specialized skill was the need for good communication through the Signal Corps. The need for expertise in this area led Gordon's dad, Robert Laymon, to volunteer despite the fact that he left a wife and three sons at home. Robert served in the South Pacific and was among those who often went in ahead of the main invasion force, using stealth tactics to string cable wire to provide communication on or between islands. Gordon Laymon, Robert's son, served our nation during the Korean War. Gordon followed in the footsteps of his father, serving in the Signal Corps for two years during that war.

Our eldest son Aaron graduated from high school in May of 2000. Shortly after graduation, Aaron came home and announced that he had joined the Army. Some of the family were upset that Aaron had joined the service. I was concerned but not in any way upset. I congratulated Aaron on joining the Army and explained to him that I felt that there was a void in my life by not having served our nation in the military. Aaron served three years active duty and spent one of those years in Korea, just south of the 38th parallel near the DMZ. After Aaron's three years of active duty service, he reenlisted in the Indiana National Guard. Just about the time his National Guard service was to expire, Aaron's group was called up for a tour to Iraq, where he spent a year in the Ramadi region outside Baghdad. Upon Aaron's return from Iraq, he reenlisted again for another term in the Indiana National Guard. It now appears that Aaron's group will be called up to Afghanistan in 2010 or 2011.

Each of the men above were willing to do whatever was asked of them to defend Liberty and Freedom; not just for America, but quite literally for all mankind around the world. *"We the People"* owe these men, and other Americans just like them, a huge debt of gratitude.

From the United States Constitution

*"**We the People** of the United States, in Order to form a more perfect Union, establish Justice, insure domestic Tranquility, **provide for the common defense**, promote the general Welfare, and secure the Blessings of Liberty to ourselves and our Posterity, do ordain and establish this Constitution for the United States of America."*

One of the few legitimate purposes, and certainly ***the*** single most important purpose for, and responsibility of, the United States federal government is to ***"provide for the common defense"*** of the nation of the United States. The military comprises between 25 percent and 50 percent of total spending by the federal government, depending upon how you choose to allocate interest on the federal debt, veterans' benefits, military pensions, and so on. ***Direct*** military costs are 20 percent to 25 percent of the total annual U.S. federal budget. In the reorganization of the government, there will be the same thorough top-to-bottom review of effectiveness and efficiencies related to military spending that should always accompany any reorganization. Changes should include a revisit of where the United States military is stationed overseas and why they are stationed in each of these foreign lands. The United States will always come to the aid of her friends and will most certainly always protect her interests, both foreign and domestic.

However, from this day forward, she can no longer afford, nor should others any longer look for her, to serve as the "military police" for the world. The United States government continues to have 70,000 military personnel stationed in Germany <u>alone</u>. World War II ended sixty-four years ago. It is time to bring most all of these troops home. ***"We the People"*** of the United States are now in the process of learning to face our inherent limitations and to live within our "collective means" as a nation. The United States can no longer afford to protect the world militarily. The U.S. military establishment cannot and will not be exempt from the financial austerity that our entire nation must now endure. However, cuts in the Defense Department will not come from the troops or military readiness but rather from the endless waste that our present group of corrupt, career, elitist politicians have inappropriately buried in the Defense budget. A great example would be the recent purchase of the Gulfstream jets for members of Congress to fly around in.

> *"By calling attention to 'a well-regulated militia,' the 'security' of the nation, and the right of each citizen 'to keep and bear arms,' our founding fathers recognized the essentially civilian nature of our economy. Although it is extremely unlikely that the fears of governmental tyranny, which gave rise to the Second Amendment, will ever be a major danger to our nation, the amendment still remains an important declaration of our basic civilian-military relationships, in which every citizen must be ready to participate in the defense of his country.*
> *For that reason, I believe the Second Amendment will always be important."*
> **—Senator John F. Kennedy, 1960**

This quote by Senator, and soon to be President, John F. Kennedy is in support of the Second Amendment to the U.S. Constitution. Isn't it interesting that fifty years ago, J.F.K.'s quote includes a reference to the amendment in which his perception was that *"it is extremely unlikely that the fears of governmental tyranny, which gave rise to the Second Amendment, will ever be a major danger to our nation"* yet in our America of today in the year 2009, gun and ammunition manufacturers can't keep pace with the demand for either of these items? In his quote from 1960, Senator Kennedy makes it clear that the right to bear arms under the Second Amendment was given so that the people could protect themselves *"from fears of governmental tyranny."* This is an important admission by a Senator, and soon to be President, of the United States. Thomas Jefferson, one of the original revolutionaries, had a clear understanding of the true purpose for the Second Amendment and had this to say about it:

"The strongest reason for people to retain the right to keep and bear arms is, as a last resort, to protect themselves against tyranny in government."

—Thomas Jefferson

In our 222-year history as a nation, *"We the People"* have never taken up arms against our government (with the exception of the Civil War, an event that many founders feared might take place). This fact is an awesome testament to our form of government and to the founders who created our great Republic. Nevertheless, it doesn't hurt for our current elected leaders to be reminded, and to fully understand, that the people have the right under our Constitution to protect themselves against a tyrannical government. The recent skyrocketing sale of both guns and ammunition should give anyone serving in government pause as they go about the "people's" business. The weapons and ammunition mentioned above were not bought this past year by the American people for protection against any sort of "foreign enemy." Americans continue to be an independent people who, by and large, deeply value their Liberty, their rights, and their Freedoms, which are given them under our Constitution. Any person, or any governmental body of people, who attempt to threaten or even to ponder threatening those

Liberties, rights, and Freedoms *"of the people"* would do well to remember and to continually bear in mind this 222-year-old right of ***"We the People"*** in America.

As we transition back to a truly free society from our current status as a socialist state, and begin living within our means, we will out of necessity be required to carefully consider how our military dollars are spent. First and foremost, the federal government's responsibility is to protect the American people. In this regard, we can and must improve our intelligence gathering, especially in light of the enemies that we now face. On this matter, we can learn a great deal from our Israeli friends. Since its creation more than sixty years ago, Israel has found it essential to be incredibly resourceful—simply to survive. They are a tiny nation and are completely surrounded by much larger nations who would like nothing more than to see them disappear. Consequently, Israel has developed a very sophisticated intelligence apparatus. Israel is a friend of the United States. We need to study and learn all that we can from them. We must pull in our horns and be less interventionist. This is not to say that we should be isolationist; however, in the future, we must be more careful in picking our battles and "entangling" ourselves in the affairs of other nations. Thomas Jefferson on March 4, 1801, urged that the United States must have ***"Peace, commerce, and honest friendship with all nations—entangling alliances with none."*** His words are as true today as they were then. Who knows, perhaps if we had been more successful at national intelligence prior to 2001, we could have avoided the attacks of 9/11 by having knocked out Osama bin Laden when we had the chance, for bin Laden was at war with us well in advance of 9/11.

Solutions for a more peaceful world and a more secure America:

1. Immediately bring as many of our military personnel home from the soil of foreign nations as is possible within the confines of maintaining the security of the United States.
2. Close as many military bases in foreign nations as is possible within the same confines as above.
3. Redeploy the troops from above within the United States in order to secure our borders and to protect the sovereignty of the United States.
4. Immediately put all foreign nations on notice that the United States will no longer be serving as the "policeman of the world."
5. Immediately cease and desist from providing aid to foreign nations, explaining that we are broke.
6. Begin immediately beefing up our national intelligence community to better protect the United States from all enemies, both foreign and domestic.

Chapter Seven
Freedom, Liberty, and Ronald Reagan

Timing Is Everything

President Ronald Reagan understood what a tremendous gift our founders had given us. Reagan was a student of the founding fathers. He knew how they thought and he understood what their intentions were for this, our great democratic experiment. Reagan earnestly desired that our nation would one day turn back to and embrace the fundamental principles of our founders. Ronald Reagan was a true American patriot. While Reagan was on the right track, it turned out that he was just a little ahead of his time. In 1980, the country had not yet wandered far enough away from our founders' principles, nor had its people suffered enough pain and discomfort to arouse the masses into taking action. That has all now changed—what a difference thirty years can make. *"We the People"* are now *forced* to make a choice. Here, Reagan gives us a chilling reminder of our duties:

"Freedom is never more than one generation away from extinction. We didn't pass it to our children in the bloodstream. It must be fought for, protected, and handed on to them to do the same, or one day we will spend our sunset years telling our children and our children's children what it was once like in the United States where men were free."
—**Ronald Reagan,** fortieth President of the United States, from 1981 to 1989

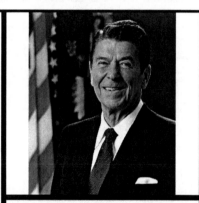

Ronald Reagan, 1911-2004

What Choice Will You Make?

We now find ourselves at a critical juncture, an important moment of decision in our nation's history. We can ignore our mistakes of the past and continue marching down the road to socialism **or** we can stop, **seriously reflect upon what we are about to give up**, and change our course back to one of Liberty and Freedom. Making the latter choice will mean that we are choosing to honor the sacrifices of our founders. It is, in the view of your author, the correct choice and the choice that I fervently hope we will make as a nation. I know for a certainty it is the choice Ronald Reagan would make. It is also the choice that will require courage and a commitment by *each of us* to once again become involved and to take an active role to help chart a course for our nation's future.

Continuing the march down the road to socialism is the easy choice and the lazy way out. It is also the choice that we have actually already made "by default" up to now, through our *apathy* and *complacency*. So doing nothing has actually been a choice by us; a very real and clear choice. Whether conscious or not, that choice has been one of willingly relinquishing our nation to the hands of people who desire to convert it to a socialist state. So this is your wake-up call. This is your last chance to redeem this great nation. What choice will *you* make?

As you consider your choice, please bear in mind that Liberty, once lost, can never be regained:

> *"A Constitution of Government once changed from Freedom, can never be restored. Liberty, once lost, is lost forever."* —**John Adams** to Abigail Adams, 1775

John Adams and Thomas Jefferson Ended Life as Devoted Correspondents:

John Adams and Thomas Jefferson had been fierce political opponents during the early years of our Republic. Jefferson believed staunchly in protecting States' rights, while Adams was a devoted Federalist. Fortunately, the two reconciled in 1812. As Adams put it: *"You and I ought not to die before we have explained ourselves to each other."* They spent the rest of their lives writing fascinating letters back and forth. Remarkably, *both* men died on the exact *same* day, *July 4, 1826*, the fiftieth anniversary to the day of their both having signed the Declaration of Independence.

John Adams, 1735–1826 Second President of the United States and longest living ex-President until Ronald Reagan died at age 93 in 2004.

Ronald Reagan and Lady Margaret Thatcher of Great Britain were great friends and political soulmates. They both governed during the same decade of the 1980s. Lady Thatcher, like Reagan, had a keen sense of humor. Perhaps this quote by Margaret Thatcher would help explain their affinity one for the other:

"The problem with socialism is that you eventually run out of other people's money."

—**Margaret Thatcher**

British Prime Minister
—1979 to 1990

"There are a thousand hacking at the branches of evil to one who is striking at the roots."

—**Henry David Thoreau**
(1817–1862)

Why a separate chapter on President Ronald Reagan? Simply because many folks reading this book will have a personal memory of Ronald Reagan and can therefore ***relate*** to what he said and did. Reagan governed during "our time." This experience allows the reader to easily validate the ideals and principles held by our founders, because Reagan's governance was consistent with these original ideals and principles of our founders. The ideals and principles that our founders used in creating our great nation are **unchanging** and **timeless**. Reagan had "internalized" their lessons. Your author considers Ronald Reagan to be America's **last true patriot statesman**.

Below are several other favorite quotes from our late and beloved Ronald Reagan:

"Here's my strategy on the Cold War: We win, they lose."

"The most terrifying words in the English language are: I'm from the government and I'm here to help."

"The trouble with our liberal friends is not that they're ignorant; it's just that they know so much that isn't so."

"Of the four wars in my lifetime, none came about because the U.S. was too strong."

"I have wondered at times about what the Ten Commandments would have looked like if Moses had run them through the U.S. Congress."

"The taxpayer: That's someone who works for the federal government but doesn't have to take the civil service examination."

"Government is like a baby: An alimentary canal with a big appetite at one end and no sense of responsibility at the other."

"The nearest thing to eternal life we will ever see on this earth is a government program."

"It has been said that politics is the second oldest profession. I have learned that it bears a striking resemblance to the first."

"Government's view of the economy could be summed up in a few short phrases: If it moves, tax it. If it keeps moving, regulate it. And if it stops moving, subsidize it."

"Politics is not a bad profession. If you succeed, there are many rewards; if you disgrace yourself, you can always write a book."

"No arsenal, or no weapon in the arsenals of the world, is as formidable as the will and moral courage of free men and women."

"If we ever forget that we're one nation under God, then we will be a nation gone under."

"If we lose Freedom here, there is no place to escape to. This is the last stand on Earth."

Reagan also liked to say:

"It is amazing how much you can accomplish if you don't care who gets the credit."

Other thoughts by our founders, forefathers, and great thinkers that are worth remembering:

"The issue today is the same as it has been throughout all history, whether man shall be allowed to govern himself or be ruled by a small elite."
—Thomas Jefferson

"The greatest tyrannies are always perpetrated in the name of the noblest causes."
—Thomas Paine

"God grants Liberty only to those who love it, and are always ready to guard and defend it."
—Daniel Webster, 1834

"The tyranny of a principal in an oligarchy is not so dangerous to the public welfare as the apathy of a citizen in a democracy."
—Montesquieu, 1748

"Tyranny is always better organized than Freedom."
—**Charles Peguy**

"The ignorance of one voter in a democracy impairs the security of all."
—**John F. Kennedy**, 1963

"In the end, more than they wanted Freedom, they wanted security. They wanted a comfortable life, and they lost it all—security, comfort, and Freedom. When ... the Freedom they wished for was Freedom from responsibility, then Athens ceased to be free."
—**Sir Edward Gibbon** (1737–1794)

"The two enemies of the people are criminals and government, so let us tie the second down with the chains of the Constitution so the second will not become the legalized version of the first."
—**Thomas Jefferson**

"I believe there are more instances of the abridgement of Freedoms of the people by gradual and silent encroachment of those in power than by violent and sudden usurpations."
—**James Madison**

"There is no nation on earth powerful enough to accomplish our overthrow ... Our destruction, should it come at all, will be from another quarter. From the inattention of the people to the concerns of their government, from their carelessness and negligence, I must confess that I do apprehend some danger. I fear that they may place too implicit a confidence in their public servants, and fail properly to scrutinize their conduct; that in this way they may be made the dupes of designing men, and become the instruments of their own undoing."
—**Daniel Webster**, June 1, 1837

"If once [the people] become inattentive to the public affairs, you and I, and Congress and Assemblies, Judges and Governors, shall all become wolves. It seems to be the law of our general nature, in spite of individual exceptions."
—**Thomas Jefferson** to Edward Carrington, 1787

"A society that puts equality ... ahead of Freedom will end up with neither."
—**Milton Friedman**

"Enlightened statesmen will not always be at the helm."
—James Madison

"Liberty is one of the most precious gifts heaven has bestowed upon Man. No treasures the earth contains or the sea conceals can be compared to it. For Liberty one can rightfully risk one's life."
—Miguel Cervantes, 1547–1616

"One man with courage makes a majority."
—Andrew Jackson, 1832

"Liberty means responsibility. That is why most men dread it."
—George Bernard Shaw, *Maxims for Revolutions*, 1903

"In matters of principle, stand like a rock."
—Thomas Jefferson

We can **all** agree that there is tremendous wisdom in the foregoing statements from these leaders and thinkers. The question is whether **"*We the People*"** can glean the lessons from the above wisdom and apply them appropriately to save our American Republic.

Chapter Eight
Immigration—Legal and Illegal

Theodore Roosevelt

Born in 1858

Died in 1919

Twenty-sixth President of the United States

Served as President of the United States from 1901 to 1909

"The things that will destroy America are prosperity at any price, peace at any price, safety first instead of duty first, the love of soft living, and the get-rich-quick theory of life."

Teddy Roosevelt

January 17, 1917

Theodore Roosevelt on immigrants and becoming an AMERICAN:

"In the first place we should insist that if the immigrant who comes here in good faith becomes an American and assimilates himself to us, he shall be treated on an exact equality with everyone else, for it is an outrage to discriminate against any such man because of creed, or birthplace, or origin. But this is predicated upon the man's becoming in very fact an American and nothing but an American... There can be no divided allegiance here. Any man who says he is an American, but something else also, isn't an American at all. We have room for but one flag, the American flag, and this excludes the red flag, which symbolizes all wars against liberty and civilization, just as much as it excludes any foreign flag of a nation to which we are hostile... We have room for but one language here, and that is the English language... and we have room for but one sole loyalty and that is a loyalty to the American people."

—**Theodore Roosevelt,** January 3, 1919, three days before he died.

"Americanization" was a favorite theme of Roosevelt's during his later years. He railed against **"hyphenated Americans"** and the prospect of a nation **"brought to ruins by a tangle of squabbling nationalities."** Roosevelt advocated the compulsory learning of English by every naturalized citizen. **"Every immigrant who comes here should be required within five years to learn English or to leave the country,"** Roosevelt said in a statement to *The Kansas City Star* in 1918. **"English should be the only language taught or used in the public schools."**

Roosevelt also insisted, on more than one occasion, that America had no room for what he called **"fifty-fifty allegiance."** In a speech made in 1917, Roosevelt said, **"It is our boast that we admit the immigrant to full fellowship and equality with the native-born. In return we demand that he shall share our undivided allegiance to the one flag which floats over all of us."**

Teddy Roosevelt was President during the beginning of the "Progressive Era" in American political thinking. He was something of a living contradiction. His party affiliation was Republican, and yet he was the President who began big government intervention in society and into the lives of the people in a significant way. He decided that big business was bad for America and became known as a "trust buster." Teddy Roosevelt felt that private property rights should ultimately be subject to the good of society and its control, and not simply subject to the rights of the property owner who had worked to acquire it. He was in favor of a progressive income tax before we ever had one. He was in favor of setting aside millions of acres of government land for the "common good." Teddy Roosevelt was an activist leader and an extremely energetic person. When he had a "falling out" with the Republican Party, he formed a third party, the Progressive or "Bull Moose" party, and Roosevelt came closer to winning a presidential election under a third party than has anyone before or since, earning 27 percent of the total vote.

Isn't it interesting that Teddy Roosevelt was "progressive" and "liberal" in so many ways, yet he was what can only be described as extremely conservative when it came to his views on immigration? No one can argue that Teddy Roosevelt wasn't a true American Patriot and a protector of our American sovereignty. Your author would not have agreed with much of Teddy Roosevelt's domestic political views; however, your author firmly believes that Teddy Roosevelt was *"right on"* when it came to his approaches and views on immigration.

Most Americans firmly believe in immigration. In a very real sense, we are **all** immigrants by virtue of the fact that none of us have to count back very many generations before we find our heritage or "roots" in another land. Our history is in many ways defined by the concept of the "melting pot," and in many respects our diversity is what helped make America so strong. In fact, many of our founders commented on this after they successfully wrote the U.S. Constitution. They all marveled that they were able to bring together so diverse a group of people and hammer out a document to form a nation that got its power from one single, united people—a uniquely "<u>American</u>" people. So while most Americans firmly believe in immigration, it is also true that most Americans firmly believe in enforcing the laws of the United States. Enforcing laws is where the real problem resides on the issue of immigration, and isn't this really what Teddy Roosevelt was saying in his approach to handling immigrants? ***"We welcome all newcomers so long as they become in every way an American. There can be no divided or 'fifty-fifty' allegiance."*** We didn't have the huge and pervasive problem of "illegal" immigration in Teddy Roosevelt's day. If it had been a problem in his day, I can just see the old "Rough Rider" perched on top of a 700-mile fence with rifle in hand. Teddy Roosevelt would have been leading the charge on solving this issue.

Solutions to the Illegal Immigration Issue:

1. **Enforce our laws.** No more amnesty. We have perfect proof that this concept doesn't work. It was 1986 when Ronald Reagan signed on to this idea. Were he living today, Reagan would be the first to say that "killing them with kindness" was obviously <u>not</u> the answer. It was a kind and generous American gesture of goodwill, but the kindness wasn't reciprocated. There is no reason to stick our hand back into that buzz saw. We all have compassion for the plight of people everywhere in the world living in poor conditions; however, that compassion cannot be used as a reason to ignore our laws and, more importantly, to discriminate against those immigrants who are patiently waiting in line to become Americans by following the rules that are clearly set out for them to follow. Allowing illegal immigrants a "free pass" to jump ahead in the line is outright discrimination against those who are following the laws, and it doesn't say much about American ethics or fairness. So from now on, if you are caught here illegally, you will be immediately taken back home. If your children were born here to you while you were an illegal alien and ***they*** are therefore also American citizens, you had better have someone in mind who is living here legally to leave them with and to care for them, or you will be taking them "home" with you under ***their*** dual citizenship status. Sorry, but using innocent children to break United States laws will no longer be tolerated nor allowed in America.

2. **Truly secure the borders.** No half measures here. No more unfulfilled promises of starting a fence and not finishing a fence. If we can send men back and forth to the moon and create missile defense systems in outer space, then we can secure our borders. *Finish the fence.* Put high-tech surveillance equipment on the border to monitor every movement. If required, put a sentry from the National Guard on top of the fence every thousand yards with tranquilizing darts. We can then help these folks "wake up at home" by dragging them back across the border while they are "sleeping it off." Before long, they will all want to get in line with the other folks who are following the rules. Now to be fair, I don't mean exactly that; however, I do mean something that will yield precisely that result.

3. **No more tolerance on divided allegiance.** English is spoken in America. Learn it and learn it fast. When you are in public, speak *only* English. In other words, when in Rome, do as the Romans do. No more voice mails in foreign languages. No more product instructions in seven foreign languages. No more press 1 for Spanish, 2 for French, 3 for German, 4 for English. All public signs are to be in English. The only exception to public signs being in a foreign language will be the signs that we supply to Mexico for their side of the border warning their residents of the tranquilizing darts that await them. How can we expect immigrants to assimilate if we make it okay for them to maintain their "old country" heritage? No, let's be clear; immigrants must become *"in every way"* an American.

There is much more to this immigration issue than just fairness. Fairness is reason enough to finally enforce our laws and do the right thing as outlined above; however, what we must also face is that _**we are broke**_. Americans spend billions of dollars in medical costs, education, and social programs on illegal aliens every year. This is money that we don't have and must therefore borrow in the names of our children and grandchildren. But then that's really a fairness issue in itself, right? It is unfair to indenture our future American generations. America is spending an average of $300 per week on unemployment benefits for each unemployed American. Let's employ Americans in the jobs that illegal immigrants are holding. If not, in a very real sense, U.S. taxpayers are paying the illegals' wages.

Chapter Nine
Faith of Our Founding Fathers

First Amendment to the U.S. Constitution:

Congress shall make no law respecting an establishment of religion, or prohibiting the free exercise thereof; or abridging the freedom of speech, or of the press; or the right of the people peaceably to assemble, and to petition the Government for a redress of grievances.

To those who would choose to separate God from America, I can only say good luck to you. Since the early days of America's founding, there has been a vigorous ongoing discussion and debate about the separation of church and state. To your author, the issue is not that difficult. Yes, I believe that the founders **did** intend to separate the church from the state. However, our founders never actually used those exact words. Those words came along later as *"We the People"* were arguing over what the founders intended. Our nation's founders were very clear. They simply did not want any particular religion, church, or denomination to dominate the public debate or to be considered **the** faith of America or **the** faith of her people. There can really be no other way of interpreting what they meant when they spelled it out for us in the First Amendment to the U.S. Constitution in our bill of rights as shown above.

Why do we need to make this subject so complicated? The founders were **very** clear—Congress would not "establish" a religion for us nor would it "prohibit" us from exercising our own choice of religion or faith. Our founders were all about **Freedom**. It should also be pointed out that while our founders made certain that *"We the People"* would have Freedom **of** religion, this in no way implies that they desired that we have Freedom **from** religion. The evidence is actually quite to the contrary. What cannot be left open to debate is whether or not the majority of our founders believed that there is a Divine Creator, a God. On that subject there can be little doubt.

Surely no thinking person can make a serious argument that the founders wanted to separate God from America. If that is a debate anyone desires to have, they are about 233 years too late. The founders **all** acknowledged that there is a Divine Creator, a God, by their very act of signing the Declaration of Independence. In fact, there is nothing that the founders desired to be clearer about than our connection to God, our Creator. After all, they put it in the first two sentences of the first two paragraphs of their Declaration of Independence. They then hung their entire right to make a separation from Great Britain on their having been given that very choice to do so **_by God_**. No, the debate of America's connection to God was fought and won <u>in God's favor</u> **before** July 4, 1776. Our founders wanted to leave no doubt about their collective belief in God. The entire essence for the existence of the United States is predicated upon our collective belief in God and with it our unalienable rights, as given by God, to life, Liberty, and the pursuit of happiness. When our rights were described as unalienable by our founders, they were specific in using that term, which means rights that cannot be separated from us, given to us, or taken away from us, by anyone **other than God.** They are "natural rights." To our founders, government's only real purpose was to protect people from losing these "natural rights" of man that were given them by God.

From the second paragraph of America's Declaration of Independence:

"We hold these truths to be self-evident, that all men are created equal, that they are endowed by their Creator with certain unalienable Rights, that among these are Life, Liberty and the pursuit of Happiness. That to secure these rights, Governments are instituted among Men, deriving their just powers from the consent of the governed ..."

Yes, our founders believed in God. One can find evidence of this everywhere. The following is just a sampling:

George Washington:
"...Reason and experience both forbid us to expect that National morality can prevail in exclusion of religious principle."
"It is impossible to rightly govern the world without God and Bible."

John Adams: In a letter written to Abigail Adams on the day the Declaration was approved by Congress:

"The general principles upon which the Fathers achieved independence were the general principles of Christianity... I will avow that I believed and now believe that those general principles of Christianity are as eternal and immutable as the existence and attributes of God." "July 4th ought to be commemorated as the day of deliverance by solemn acts of devotion to God Almighty."

"Our Constitution was made only for a moral and religious people. It is wholly inadequate to the government of any other." —**John Adams,** October 11, 1798

"I have examined all religions, as well as my narrow sphere, my straightened means, and my busy life, would allow; and the result is that the Bible is the best Book in the world. It contains more philosophy than all the libraries I have seen."
—**John Adams** in a December 25, 1813 letter to Thomas Jefferson

"Without Religion this World would be something not fit to be mentioned in polite company, I mean Hell."
—**John Adams** to Thomas Jefferson, April 19, 1817

Benjamin Franklin:
"I have lived, Sir, a long time, and the longer I live, the more convincing proof I see of this truth—that God governs in the affairs of man. And if a sparrow cannot fall to the ground without his notice, is it probable that an empire can rise without His aid?"
-Constitutional Convention of 1787;
original manuscript of this speech

"Talking against religion is unchaining a tiger; the beast let loose may worry his deliverer."
-Poor Richard's Almanac, 1751

"How many observe Christ's birthday! How few, his precepts! O! 'tis easier to keep holidays than commandments."
-Poor Richard's Almanac, 1732

"In the beginning of the contest with Britain, when we were sensible of danger, we had daily prayers in this room for Divine protection. Our prayers, Sir, were heard, and they were graciously answered... Do we imagine we no longer need His assistance?"
—**Benjamin Franklin** during the Constitutional Convention, Thursday, June 28, 1787

Alexander Hamilton:
On July 12, 1804, at his death, Hamilton said, "I have a tender reliance on the mercy of the Almighty, through the merits of the Lord Jesus Christ. I am a sinner. I look to Him for mercy; pray for me."

"For my own part, I sincerely esteem it [the Constitution] a system which without the finger of God, never could have been suggested and agreed upon by such a diversity of interests."
—1787 after the Constitutional Convention

"It cannot be emphasized too clearly and too often that this nation was founded, not by religionists, but by Christians; not on religion, but on the gospel of Jesus Christ. For this very reason, peoples of other faiths have been afforded asylum, prosperity, and freedom of worship here."
—**Patrick Henry,** May 1765 Speech to the House of Burgesses

Patrick Henry was most known for his famous quote March 23, 1775: *"Give me liberty or give me death!"*

Patrick Henry:
"Orator of the Revolution" upon writing his will...
"This is all the inheritance I can give my dear family. The religion of Christ can give them one which will make them rich indeed."
—*The Last Will and Testament of **Patrick Henry***

Alexander Hamilton:
"I have carefully examined the evidences of the Christian religion, and if I was sitting as a juror upon its authenticity I would unhesitatingly give my verdict in its favor. I can prove its truth as clearly as any proposition ever submitted to the mind of man."

Thomas Jefferson:
"The doctrines of Jesus are simple, and tend to all the happiness of man."

"Of all the systems of morality, ancient or modern which have come under my observation, none appears to me so pure as that of Jesus."

"I am a real Christian, that is to say, a disciple of the doctrines of Jesus."

"God who gave us life gave us liberty. And can the liberties of a nation be thought secure when we have removed their only firm basis, a conviction in the minds of the people that these liberties are a gift from God? That they are not to be violated but with His wrath? Indeed I tremble for my country when I reflect that God is just, and that His justice cannot sleep forever." —1781

So there you have it; America's founding fathers in their own words about their own personal faith. Have you ever wondered why the United States was so blessed as a nation for so many years and was able to grow so fast and become so highly prosperous? Might this have been because **"We the People"** for the majority of our existence as a nation held true to God's simple and fundamental rules of living? If so, what happens if **"We the People"** stray from God's laws? What will become of us then? And have we already strayed? Clearly, that is what Jefferson feared might occur in his quote above. Jefferson warned us that God's **"justice cannot sleep forever."** He reminded us that our Liberty was a gift from God and that **"We the People"** must never forget this truth. The good news is that if we have strayed, there **is** hope for God's people:

From the Bible, 2nd Chronicles 7:14:

"If my people, which are called by my name, shall humble themselves, and pray, and seek my face, and turn from their wicked ways; then will I hear from heaven, and will forgive their sin, and will heal their land."

All of the founders quoted above have made writing this chapter, and indeed the writing of this entire book, a very easy task for your author. After all, why make an argument in your own words when those who have come before you have already made the same argument so much more eloquently, convincingly, and succinctly than your own poor ability to add or detract from the effort? Your author would be remiss, however, if I didn't make known my own beliefs on faith. Therefore, allow me to state unequivocally that I, like Thomas Jefferson, consider myself to be as Jefferson said: **"A real Christian, that is to say, a disciple of the doctrines of Jesus."**

Chapter Ten
What Would Our Founding Fathers Do?

> **A Nine (9) Point Plan to Save America from an otherwise Certain Demise.**

The Nine (9) Specific Goals of _**The 2nd American Revolution**_ are:

1. To peacefully remove as many of the 535 incumbent members of the U.S. Congress from office as is possible on November 2, 2010, and elect **"citizen"** statesmen, thus forming a **people's** Congress to enact…much-needed reforms and changes.

2. To institute sweeping changes in the federal government that include substantially reducing its size and scope over three to five years, beginning immediately with the elimination of the Departments of Education, Agriculture, Labor, and so on (the list is long), transferring any and all required functions of government to the lowest possible level in our society (villages, municipalities, towns, cities, townships, counties, and states, in that order). To repeal the $700 billion TARP legislation of October 2008 and the $787 billion economic stimulus bill passed in February of 2009, and so on.

3. To begin immediately, in very early 2011, the liquidation of U.S. government assets including real estate, vehicle fleets, all equity ownership stakes in any U.S. corporations such as General Motors, Chrysler, AIG, and Citigroup, selling these assets back to the private sector and using the funds to start paying down the U.S. national debt, beginning first with any and all debt held by foreigners and foreign nations.

4. To immediately, in very early 2011, call for the passage by the U.S. Congress of an amendment to the U.S. Constitution requiring term limits for _**all**_ federal officials.

5. To immediately, in very early 2011, call for the passage by the U.S. Congress of an amendment to the U.S. Constitution requiring a balanced U.S. federal budget.

6. To immediately, in very early 2011, call for the passage by the U.S. Congress of an amendment to the U.S. Constitution providing for a presidential line item veto.

7. To totally **repeal** the Sixteenth Amendment to the U.S. Constitution passed in 1913, which allows the federal government to tax individual citizens on their incomes.

8. *"We the People."* do hereby put the United States Congress and the U.S. President on notice that they are to immediately ***cease and desist*** from any further "nationalization" of the private sector of the U.S. economy or intervention into the lives and property of *"We the People."*

9. To inspire, educate, and motivate the electorate, inciting them to ***thought*** and to ***action***.

See a summary of each of these nine (9) goals throughout this chapter in the pages that follow. For a complete discussion of *The 2ⁿᵈ American Revolution*, please read the entire book.

Goal #1

> To peacefully remove as many of the 535 incumbent members of the U.S. Congress from office as is possible on November 2, 2010, and elect *"citizen"* statesmen, thereby forming a *people's* Congress to enact much-needed reforms and changes.

There can be little doubt that we will see an unprecedented change in the make-up of the U.S. Congress after the elections of November 2, 2010. What is ***not*** clear is whether *"We the People"* will replace ***enough*** of the Congress to be able to bring about the level of change that is desperately needed in America. This chapter of your book reviews the number of *"citizen"* statesmen that need to be elected as well as the election process required to get them elected in order to return Liberty and Freedom to the American people. This goal is #1 because the entire hope for regaining America and honoring the sacrifices of our founders hinges on this #1 goal. If *"We the People"* can change the Congress, then *"We the People"* can change the nation.

"The power under the Constitution will always be with the people. It is entrusted for certain defined purposes, and for a certain limited period, to representatives of their own choosing; and whenever it is executed contrary to their interest, or not agreeable to their wishes, their servants can, and undoubtedly will, be recalled."

George Washington, 1787
First President of the United States and "Father of Our Country"

Goal #2

To institute sweeping changes in the federal government that include substantially reducing its size and scope over three to five years, beginning immediately with the elimination of the Departments of Education, Agriculture, Labor, and so on (the list is long), transferring any and all required functions of government to the lowest possible level in our society (villages, municipalities, towns, cities, townships, counties, and states, in that order). To repeal the $700 billion TARP legislation of October 2008 and the $787 billion economic stimulus bill passed in February of 2009, and so on.

What we now know for a certainty is that our elected leaders are incompetent and have proven that they are completely incapable of solving the problems that confront our great nation. If these people were officers running a major corporation, they would all have been terminated long ago by the shareholders for dereliction of their duties. Well, guess what? *"We the People"* **are** the shareholders of America and the time has arrived for *"We the People"* to fire the current management of the U.S. government. The list of their abuses is as long as those made against King George and the British Parliament during the 1ˢᵗ American Revolution. In many respects, their abuses and usurpations are actually **more** heinous. *"We the People"* will now have to "undo" much of the harm these folks have done to our great nation.

"A little matter will move a party, but it must be something great that moves a nation."
—**Thomas Paine,** *Rights of Man,* 1792
Born in England in 1737—Died in America in 1809

Goal #3

To begin immediately, in very early 2011, the liquidation of U.S. government assets including real estate, vehicle fleets, all equity ownership stakes in any U.S. corporations such as General Motors, Chrysler, AIG, and Citigroup, selling these assets back to the private sector and using the funds to start paying down the U.S. national debt beginning first with any and all debt held by foreigners and foreign nations.

America is financially bankrupt. Absent liquidation, downsizing, and reorganization of the U.S. government, the reckless actions of our government will soon lead to the demise of the United

States through the relinquishment of our sovereignty to foreigners and the destruction of our currency. This is totally unacceptable. Therefore, *"We the People"* will now be taking matters into our own hands. We will immediately begin to put the affairs of the United States into order.

"As a very important source of strength and security, cherish public credit. One method of preserving it is to use it as sparingly as possible."
—**George Washington,**
President of the United States
From his Farewell Address,
September 17, 1796
Born in 1732, Washington died in 1799

"Government is not reason; it is not eloquent; it is force. Like fire, it is a dangerous servant and a fearful master."

George Washington

"To contract new debts is not the way to pay old ones."
—**George Washington** to James Welch, April 7, 1799

Goal #4

To immediately, in very early 2011, call for the passage by the U.S. Congress of an Amendment to the U.S. Constitution requiring term limits for __all__ federal officials.

Many of the problems that plague the United States of America stem from the corruption in our political system. The most egregious corruption has come about as a direct result of allowing elected officials to remain in office for extended periods and to be bought and sold by lobbyists and special interest groups. Washington, D.C., has become nothing more than a swamp, a cesspool of greed and corruption. The time has come for *"We the People"* to drain the swamp, to clean the cesspool. Once *"We the People"* have swept the majority of our current U.S. Congress from office, the new *"people's"* Congress will pass an amendment to the U.S. Constitution limiting the number of terms elected officials may remain in office. This will cleanse the system and serve to bring the *"fresh ideas"* that are desperately needed. All federal judges, including the Supreme Court Justices, will be subject to reconfirmation each nine years.

"To prevent every danger which might arise to American freedom from continuing too long in office, it is earnestly recommended that we set an obligation on the holder of that office to go out after a certain period."
—Thomas Jefferson

Goal #5

To immediately, in very early 2011, call for the passage by the U.S. Congress of an amendment to the U.S. Constitution requiring a balanced U.S. federal budget each year.

In an abundance of caution, as well as to never again suffer the risk of losing our nation or its sovereignty, the new *"people's"* Congress will pass an amendment to the U.S. Constitution requiring that the United States federal government perpetually maintain a balanced budget each and every fiscal year. As an additional limit on the federal government, federal spending shall be limited to 20 percent of GDP. The only exception to these requirements will be in the event of a declared war and then only if the U.S. Congress, not the U.S. President, declares that war. Forty-nine (49) states have this requirement. It is now time the federal government does as well.

"I wish it were possible to obtain a single amendment to our Constitution.
I would be willing to depend on that alone for the reduction of the administration of our government to the genuine principles of its Constitution; I mean an additional article, taking from the federal government the power of borrowing."
—**Thomas Jefferson,** in a letter to John Taylor, November 26, 1798

Goal #6

To immediately, in very early 2011, call for the passage by the U.S. Congress of an amendment to the U.S. Constitution providing for a presidential line item veto.

Again, in an abundance of caution, *"We the People"* must be prudent going forward in curbing the power, scope, and spending of the federal government. A presidential line item veto will be a great aid in restraining the Congress from their inherent natural tendency to overspend. History has proven that elected officials cannot be trusted as good stewards of the *"people's"* money, for as Davey Crockett said in the 1830s, *"Money with them is nothing but trash when it is to come out of the people. But it is the one great thing for which most of them are striving, and many of them sacrifice honor, integrity, and justice to obtain it."* There is no downside risk to our nation in providing the president a hand in limiting the fiscal excesses of the Congress. Only this measure will bring restraint, which each of us knows has been lacking and is greatly needed. Forty-three (43) states empower their governors with this tool. Our national government now needs to honor the will of the people and provide this for our president as well.

"All men having power ought to be mistrusted."
—**James Madison,** fourth President of the United States of America, President during the years 1809 to 1817

Considered the "Father of the Constitution" as well as the "Father of the Bill of Rights"

Goal #7

> To totally **repeal** the Sixteenth Amendment to the U.S. Constitution passed in 1913, which allows the federal government to tax individual citizens on their incomes.

Once the size and scope of the U.S. government has been significantly reduced by the new *"people's"* Congress; a significant amount of the United States national debt has been paid; term limits, balanced budget, and presidential line item veto amendments are all passed, ratified, and in place, it will no longer be necessary for *"We the People"* to pay taxes on individual income to the federal treasury. It would be fitting and proper to pass this new amendment, which repeals the 16th Amendment, on February 3, 2013: **one hundred years to the day after** the Sixteenth Amendment was ratified. This will end a hundred-year-old battle over the constitutionality and the legality of that amendment.

> *"A government big enough to give you everything you want, is big enough to take away everything you have."*
> —**Gerald Ford,** President of the United States, before Congress
> August 12, 1974
>
> The above quote has often been attributed to Thomas Jefferson; however, there has been no evidence found that Thomas Jefferson actually ever made this quote.

Goal #8

> *"We the People"* do hereby put the United States Congress and the U.S. President on notice that they are to immediately **_cease and desist_** from any further "nationalization" of the private sector of the U.S. economy or intervention into the lives and property of *"We the People."*

In just the past few months, the so-called representatives of the people in the United States government have piled many times more debt onto the backs of the American people than the

United States accumulated during the ***entire*** first two centuries of its existence. They did this in clear defiance of ***"We the People"*** as we began saying **NO** to their $700 billion TARP legislation. The representatives then started nationalizing entire segments of the U.S. economy, including banking, insurance, and automobiles. Now these so-called representatives are determined to do a takeover and nationalization of the entire United States health care industry. **So:** No more new stimulus packages. No more nationalizing private companies or industries. The plate of the ***2011 People's*** Congress is already full of legislation and spending that they must begin repealing. Therefore, ***"We the People" of the United States hereby demand that the United States Congress and the President of the United States immediately cease and desist from any further nationalization of the private sector of the U.S. economy and that they do not further intervene or entangle the government into the lives or property of "We the People" until at least such time as the 112th Congress convenes on January 3, 2011.*** In this way, ***"We the People"*** will have been given the opportunity to conduct a "national referendum" during the next national election to be held on November 2, 2010, on the merits of our current government's incessant march toward socialism. John Adams reminds us below that Liberty is fragile and that once lost, is lost forever.

John Adams & Thomas Jefferson Ended Life as Devoted Correspondents:

John Adams and Thomas Jefferson had been fierce political opponents during the early years of our Republic. Jefferson believed staunchly in protecting State's rights while Adams was a devoted Federalist. Fortunately the two reconciled in 1812. As Adams put it, ***"You and I ought not to die before we have explained ourselves to each other."*** They spent the rest of their lives writing fascinating letters back and forth. Remarkably, **both** men died on the **same** day, ***July 4th, 1826***, the 50th anniversary to the day of their both having signed the Declaration of Independence.

John Adams
1735–1826
Second president of the United States and longest living ex-president until Ronald Reagan died at age 93 in 2004.

"A Constitution of Government once changed from Freedom, can never be restored. Liberty, once lost, is lost forever." —**John Adams** to Abigail Adams, 1775

Goal #9

> To inspire, educate, and motivate the electorate, inciting them to **thought** and to **action**.

We have our marching orders. Our founders, in the Declaration of Independence, were very clear. All people are endowed by their Creator with certain unalienable (natural) rights, which include life, Liberty, and the pursuit of happiness. Governments are created among men as a means to protect these natural rights, and the government's power is subject to the *"consent of the people."* If and when any government becomes destructive to the natural rights of the people, it is the right, and literally, *"it is the duty"* of the people to alter, abolish, or amend that government.

So here we are—233 years after the signing of the American Declaration of Independence and 222 years after the creation of the American government under our U.S. Constitution. Has our government destroyed our natural rights? Let us review and answer that question for just the three rights *specifically* mentioned in the Declaration:

1. **Life.** Yes, very clearly, our government destroys life. The grossest example of this is on the issue of abortion. Argue what you will about when life begins. Take any side you like. With respect to our government's action, it makes no difference whether life begins at conception <u>or not</u>. What is not arguable is what our government *did* through the U.S. Supreme Court in the 1974 *Roe vs. Wade* decision. The court decided that *even if* a human fetus is alive, it *is* still okay to kill it. If the definition of when conception begins had *not* been known, and could not be determined, then the U.S. government had no right to enter the debate. Our founding fathers would very likely have said that if the moment life begins could not be determined, the government should in no way be involved in this matter. *If there were* life at conception, their decision in sanctioning abortion would frustrate the spirit under which and violate the very basis upon which our nation was founded. Abortions were occurring in America well before the U.S. government weighed in on the issue. The Supreme Court should have refused to hear the case. That is the real issue. We could now go on with stem cell and other issues, but these are moot, for abortion trumps them all.

2. **Liberty.** Yes, very clearly, our government destroys our Liberty. Since "tax Freedom day" is May 29 this year (2009), that means we must work more than 40 percent of the year just to support the U.S. government. Therefore, if government seizes five out of every twelve months of the people's labor and productivity, government is guilty of destroying the people's Liberty. Shall we bother to mention other Liberty-destroying acts by government such as their intrusive and excessive regulation or their acts of burdening future generations of Americans with *trillions* of dollars of debt, thereby enslaving them to a life of servitude? Let's not; citing May 29 above is sufficient.

3. **The Pursuit of Happiness.** Yes, very clearly, our government destroys our ability to pursue any real happiness in our lives. If happiness means having the Freedom to do with your time and your resources what you want, when you want, then working solely to support government until May 29 every year before being allowed to have any time to claim as your own pretty well frustrates anyone's ability to be happy. Under that scenario, America is really nothing more than a "forced labor camp" where working people are allowed to keep whatever is left over after the government *first* decides what *it* needs. Not much to be happy about there. Is there any reason for me to continue on? I didn't think so.

Has your author reached goal #9 yet? Are you inspired, educated, motivated to *thought* and to *action*? So far, we are three-for-three on making the case that the government has destroyed our natural, God-given rights. Is there any need to further continue down this road? Or is the verdict already in? *"We the People" must now act.* Our founders were clear. It is our right; and more importantly, *it is our duty* to act. A right is something that is optional for you to exercise, but a duty is something you are *obligated* to perform. *"We the People"* have a *duty* to set things right. We have a *duty* to do this for many reasons. If we fail to act, the very Republic for which our founders and forefathers sacrificed their lives will be lost. Besides, aren't we obligated to preserve that Republic for future generations of Americans? Yes, *"We the People"* are left with no alternative. We are *required* to act.

"Whenever the people are well informed, they can be trusted with their own government; that whenever things get so far wrong as to attract their notice, they may be relied on to set them to rights." —**Thomas Jefferson** in a letter to Richard Price, January 8, 1789

How Do *"We the People"* Fight and Win the 2ⁿᵈ American Revolution?

There are essentially three ways to peacefully accomplish the goals of *"We the People."* They are:

1. Internal reform and amendments of the Constitution by our current elected leaders.

2. Elect new national leaders who will reform the government and amend the Constitution.

3. Amend the Constitution by three-fourths of the states voting to amend it via a Constitutional Convention.

#1. This first approach is for our current elected officials in the U.S. Congress, under the leadership of the President, to propose and pass amendments to the U.S. Constitution that are desired by the people and further, to dismantle much of the federal government and evolve many of the functions that are held there back to the **local level** to individuals, communities, and local and state governments. What we already know for a certainty is that there is virtually **_no chance_** whatsoever of this occurring under our current political system. The U.S. Congress proved this when they refused to support a simple Term Limits Amendment to the U.S. Constitution in 1995.

#2. The second option is for *"We the People"* to organize at a grass-roots level county-by-county and state-by-state, vote out the current set of national leaders, and replace them with an entirely new set of *"citizen"* statesmen who will pass the Constitutional amendments that are needed and dismantle much of the federal bureaucracy. This approach has challenges, for it is difficult to rally an entire nation of people from sea to shining sea in order to accomplish these big goals. However, this solution is entirely plausible given the current state of tremendous dissatisfaction among the electorate. As was mentioned in the preface to this book, tea parties have been held all across the United States in 2009. 750 such gatherings were held on a single day—tax day, April 15, 2009. It was estimated that twice that many gatherings occurred again on July 4, 2009. Then there was the march on Washington on September 12, 2009. Literally **_hundreds of thousands, if not millions,_** of American citizens have attended these events. A like number of concerned citizens have been attending town hall meetings all across America during the hot August summer of 2009, where they have been holding our elected officials' feet to the fire concerning their desire to take over America's health care system. In our system of government, real change can be brought about in one of two ways—through the executive or the legislative branches. As it turns out, the only hope that **"We the People"** have of bringing the reforms needed within the time frame required will be through the legislature or U.S. Congress. The Congress has the ability to render the executive branch powerless simply by turning off the flow of money. Henceforth, this will be our focus.

#3. The third approach is for a Constitutional Convention to be called by the legislatures in at least two-thirds of our fifty states and for that Convention to propose various amendments to the U.S. Constitution. These amendments would then be sent to the states for approval by at least three-fourths of the fifty state legislatures. This route bypasses Congress entirely but has never been used as a means to amend the U.S. Constitution.

There is actually a fourth way to accomplish the goals of **"We the People."** That approach would be by "popular amendment." This approach is actually not even mentioned in the U.S. Constitution. Because it has never been used, it is lost to many students of the Constitution. Framer James Wilson* endorsed popular amendment, and the topic is examined at some length in Akhil Reed Amar's book, **_The Constitution: A Biography_**. The notion of popular amendment comes from the conceptual framework of the Constitution. The Constitution's power comes from the people; the people adopted it; it functions at the behest of, and for the benefit of, **the people**. Given all of this, if **"We the People,"** as a whole, demand a change to the Constitution, should not the people be allowed to make a change? Wilson noted in 1787, "**_The people may change the Constitution whenever and however they please. This is a right of which no positive institution can ever deprive them_**." It makes sense, for if the people demand a change, it should be made. In this way, the change may **not** be the will of the Congress, **nor** of the states. The two methods of amending the Constitution that are enumerated within the document might not always be practical, for they rely on these institutions. The reality is that if the people do not support the Constitution in its present form, it cannot survive. The real issue of amending the document is not in the conceptual realm, but in the practical. Since there is no process specified for "popular amendment," what would that process be? There are no national elections today. Even elections for the presidency are local. There is no precedent for a national referendum. So it is easy to say that the Constitution can be changed by the people in any way the people wish. Actually making the change becomes altogether another story. Suffice it to say, that for now, the notion of popular amendment makes perfect sense in the constitutional framework, even though the details of affecting popular amendment could be difficult to resolve. The challenge lies in getting **"We the People"** organized on a national level. While we have never held a national referendum, the time may have arrived to force this.

*1742–1798 British-born U.S. jurist. He signed the Declaration of Independence (1776), attended the Constitutional Convention in Philadelphia, and served as a justice on the U.S. Supreme Court (1789–1798).

Amending the U.S. Constitution, while rare, has been done twenty-seven times (actually only seventeen times if you consider the Bill of Rights to be just one amendment) in our history. *Serious* government reform that falls short of amending the Constitution is even rarer than that, and any *serious* attempts at reform have occurred much less often than the amendment process. As Thomas Jefferson so wisely stated in 1787, *"the natural progress of things is for Liberty to yield and government to gain ground."* His words would become truer than he or any one of our founders could have imagined. Of course, Jefferson was also the founder who called for a new revolution every ten or twenty years as a way to cleanse the political system and refresh Liberty. Jefferson warned that if **"We the People"** became lethargic, lazy, and apathetic, we would lose our Freedom. If Thomas Jefferson were alive today, there can be little doubt that he would be leading the charge for this 2ⁿᵈ American Revolution. In fact, Jefferson would very likely be telling us that **_this_** revolution is long overdue and has been about one hundred years too late in the making.

So Where Do We Go From Here?

As stated at the beginning of this book, it is the sincere hope of your author that our 2ⁿᵈ American Revolution can be fought and won not with the shedding of blood, but rather through an active and engaged electorate. Your author also stated something else at the beginning of this book that bears repeating. It is simply this: If **"We the People"** do not take our nation back, in a peaceful manner by ballot, from the current corrupt bunch to whom we have entrusted it, this does not in any way mean that we will be able to *avoid* a 2ⁿᵈ American Revolution. No, quite to the contrary; this 2ⁿᵈ American Revolution *will occur* either peacefully through **"We the People"** once again becoming engaged, __or__ it will come by staring down the barrel of a gun. The choice is ours. **"We the People"** of today have the luxury of a choice that our founders were not given. We can, we must, use ballots instead of bullets. So how do we accomplish our goals?

Option 1 is clearly out of the question and is unworkable. Option 3, while never having been used, might be the best approach. After all, it took the states to ultimately give life to the United States Constitution in the first place. A logical argument could be made that we should therefore look to the states to amend the document or to limit its power. Besides, many states have recently indicated their dissatisfaction with our federal government's actions. Several states are already organizing and debating this issue on a statewide basis. Texas Governor Rick Perry, according to the interpretations made by many different people, has gone so far as to suggest that Texas might consider once again becoming its own **_nation_** by seceding from the United States. On April 9, 2009, Governor Perry said this: ***"I believe that our federal government has become oppressive in its size, its intrusion into the lives of our citizens, and its interference with the affairs of our state. That is why I am here today to express my unwavering support for efforts all across our country to reaffirm the states' rights affirmed by the Tenth Amendment to the U.S. Constitution. I believe that returning to the letter and spirit of the U.S. Constitution and its essential Tenth Amendment will free our state from undue regulations, and ultimately strengthen our Union."***

Below are comments made by Governor Rick Perry at a tea party protest held April 15, 2009:

Governor Rick Perry

"Texas is a unique place. When we came into the Union in 1845, one of the issues was that we would be able to leave if we decided to do that.... My hope is that America and Washington in particular pays attention. We've got a great Union. There's absolutely no reason to dissolve it. But if Washington continues to thumb their nose at the American people, who knows what may come of that."

Did I hear someone say Rick Perry for President in 2012?

Texas Governor Rick Perry
Years in office-2000 to present

Below is the county-by-county electoral map from the 2004 presidential election. The shading on the map represents the way in which the counties within each state voted for President Bush and Senator Kerry. What *is not* important about this map is which candidate is represented by which shade. What *is* important about this map is the lopsided nature of the **shades** and what **that** represents. This map would argue in favor of using option 3 for Constitutional change. Why so? Option 3 makes changes to the Constitution by virtue of geography, and the outcome is determined by the sheer number of states in favor. There are fifty states in the United States. It takes thirty-three (2/3) states to call a Constitutional Convention and thirty-eight (3/4) states to vote for and ultimately to ratify any changes to the Constitution. It is highly likely that the map below illustrates some close commonalities among the people in each of the two shades. The strategy here would be to rally the folks in the states that are represented by the lighter shade that comprises 80 percent of the map and convince the people in those thirty-eight or so states to rally around the causes and issues of the 2nd American Revolution. Despite the obvious opportunity that geography represents in this map in bringing about the desired result, it will nevertheless likely be very difficult to get so large and diverse a group of people in each of these states organized simultaneously. This would probably explain why option 3 has never been used as a successful means to amend the United States Constitution. A Constitutional Convention is actually in many ways like the "popular amendment" approach.

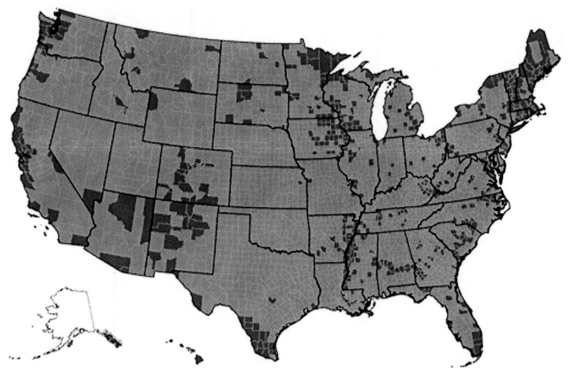

If we rule out option 1 and 3, that leaves option 2. In the thinking of your author, this is the most promising option. Option 2 is not just promising because it has been the only means by which the U.S. Constitution has been amended. Option 2 actually has the most promise because it offers the fewest hurdles to overcome, and it can be accomplished **_sooner_** than any other approach. All that is required for this option to be successful is for there to be enough frustration, pain, and suffering of **_"We the People"_** to make it work. And it sure seems that frustration, pain, and suffering are in great abundance in the United States at this particular time in our history! All that **_"We the People"_** need do to bring about the change desired is to simply **<u>NOT</u>** vote for **_any incumbent_** in both the primary and general elections of 2010. ***It's that simple!*** We simply replace at least a minimum number of representatives to effect the change desired and have them vote for that change under their mandate. It makes no difference if the incumbent elected official is your brother or best friend, he **_must_** be voted against. And frankly, if your brother or best friend were a true Patriot, he would not even seek reelection in 2010 in order to show support for his nation, knowing that his very presence in office would serve only to compromise his objectivity when voting for the changes that 80 percent of the American people want enacted. What is the magic number of new representatives required? That is a question that will be subject to much opinion and debate. However, if **_"We the People"_** can replace at least half of the representatives in both Houses of Congress with **_"citizen"_** statesmen who are committed to the principles of the 2nd American Revolution, it is the opinion of your author that it would "do the trick." Why just half, when it requires a 2/3 majority of both Houses voting in favor of any amendment to the Constitution in order to pass? Simply because at least 50 percent of the remaining "old elitist career politicians" will become swept up in the mandate for reform, thereby rendering them powerless to mount any resistance. They will simply remain there as **_"lame ducks"_** until they are "term-limited" out of office.

Conclusion

Time is of the essence. November 2, 2010, is the *"winner takes all"* election for America's future. If the American people continue their long apathetic sleep walk and lazy complacency through the 2nd of November, 2010, it is highly likely that their opportunity to redeem our nation will be forever lost. John Adams's prophetic words will then become reality for America: *"A Constitution of Government once changed from Freedom, can never be restored. Liberty, once lost, is lost forever."* This book therefore is a battle cry to you. It is your *"call to arms."* If *"We the People"* don't begin to take America back on **that day**, we may as well once and for all time wave the white flag of surrender to the socialist progressives who are bent on destroying her. This is our moment of truth. It is do or die for America and for the fundamental ideals and principles for which she was created. During the lows of the Revolutionary War, Thomas Paine wrote: *"These are the times that try men's souls. The summer soldier and the sunshine patriot will, in this crisis, shrink from the service of his country; but he that stands it now, deserves the thanks of man and woman."* Paine's words are ever truer today in **our time**.

Several friends have said to me that *"you must have a lot guts to have written that book."* Others have warned me to *"be careful, don't forget that you are in business, political topics are 'taboo' and this could cost you."* My response has been consistent and is backed by a steely resolve. The response is simply that this is not about politics. **This is about America.** When it comes to the future of America, there can be no compromise and no silence. I have learned that there are certain things in life that have a value far above money or favor. Some of those things include holding true to your convictions and your principles. I have also come to a place in my life where I must now work for causes greater than my own. For this reason, it wasn't as though I really even had a choice in writing this book. It **had** to be done. Once I truly learned and fully understood what a tremendous gift God gave us through those who have come before us, I felt it my solemn duty to do all I could to help preserve that gift, especially since that gift is under such grave threat of destruction. Besides, at least nine or ten generations before us have done the same; so it's the very **least** that I can do. Therefore, I don't mind being what Charles A. Beard described as a *"dangerous citizen."* Quite to the contrary, I wear it as a badge of honor. There is no doubt that the course I am undertaking in this effort will lead to confrontation, criticism, and possibly much worse. However, I am more than willing, in fact honored, to accept whatever befalls me as a result of this work.

It seems your author is now officially a "dangerous citizen":

"You need only reflect that one of the best ways to get yourself a reputation as a dangerous citizen these days is to go about repeating the very phrases which our founding fathers used in the struggle for independence."
—**Charles A. Beard**, American Historian
(1874–1948)

Writing this book has been one of the most meaningful and at the same time most humbling experiences of my life. During the research phase of the project, I began to really discover and to understand the sacrifices that our founders and forefathers made in creating and preserving this great nation. That experience deeply moved me. It was this awareness that kept me motivated to finish the book, for I felt an obligation to share what had been learned. Our nation's existence is nothing short of a miracle. The United States of America could not have been brought into being by random chance or through some series of "accidental" events. Our nation's existence has a significant purpose for **_all_** mankind. Our creation and survival as a nation has to have been Providential. *"We the People"* cannot, and we must not, stand idly by and watch her disappear. If you have been motivated to take any action at all as a result of your experience in reading this book, I implore you to at least, at a very minimum, commit to vote in the U.S. election of November 2, 2010. God bless each of you and may God Bless America. Your humble and obedient servant in the American cause, William E. Shuttleworth—a farmer from Indiana.

"Facts Are Stubborn Things"—John Adams, 1770

Politicians of every "stripe" have enjoyed using the above quote from John Adams, America's second president. Your author couldn't resist doing his own rendition of

"Facts Are Stubborn Things"

Fact: **Subsidize something and you get more of it. Tax something and you get less of it.** If you *subsidize* people for being dependent and non-productive, you will find them showing up in droves. If you *tax* people for being productive and hard working, you will see them fleeing like rats from a sinking ship.

Fact: **In 1820, more than 80 percent of the world's population lived in "extreme poverty."** By the year 1950, that percentage had dropped to 50 percent with very little government involvement of any kind. This was a good trend. In the United States, poverty continued to decline consistently from 1950 to 1968, and then in 1968 poverty *stopped* declining. 1968 was the year that L.B.J.'s "Great Society" began in earnest with what he described as an *"all-out war on poverty."* The United States has spent *trillions* of dollars on welfare since 1968. This second fact **proves** the first fact and the first fact **predicted** the second fact.

Fact: **There is nothing more "permanent" than a "temporary" government program**. At least that is until "the 2nd American Revolution," at which time this will *reverse*. Once "the 2nd American Revolution" war is waged and won, there will be nothing more "temporary" than a "permanent" government program.

Fact: **You cannot provide health care to <u>98</u> percent of Americans by increasing taxes on <u>2</u> percent of Americans.**

Fact: **All Americans <u>love</u> their country, but many of them are *appalled* by the behavior of her government. Just since January of 2009, the American government, by the actions of American leaders, has:**

1. Purchased controlling interests in and is operating the following private corporations: General Motors, Chrysler, AIG, Citigroup and other banks, etc.
2. Bowed to the king of Saudi Arabia
3. Told the Mexicans that their drug and violence problems are the fault of America

4. Praised the Marxist leader Daniel Ortega
5. Traveled the world apologizing to foreign nations about America's greatness
6. Offended the Queen of England
7. Released intelligence gathering secrets of America despite being warned by the CIA not to do so
8. Kissed Hugo Chavez on the cheek
9. Taken steps to nationalize the health care industry in America despite failures of Medicare, Medicaid, Social Security, etc.
10. Endorsed the Socialist Evo Morales of Bolivia
11. Increased America's national debt more in one year than America had accumulated in 200 years
12. Announced the termination of our space-based missile defense system at the same moment the North Koreans launched an intercontinental ballistic missile
13. Spent $400,000 of taxpayer money flying Air Force One over New York City, causing mass panic of America's citizens, in order to get a photo that could have been created on a computer for $1
14. Spent $787 billion of taxpayer money on foolish pork projects and called it "economic stimulus"
15. Nationalized much of America's auto, insurance, and banking industries by spending billions
16. Announced that we will meet with Iranians with no pre-conditions
17. Rushed trillions of dollars of spending bills through Congress without bothering to read them
18. Thrown a $700,000 party for employees of the Social Security Administration at the Arizona Biltmore Resort and Spa in Phoenix, as a "stress reducer" for those employees at a time when Social Security is facing **TRILLIONS** of dollars in debt and unfunded pension liabilities
19. Appointed citizens of America to the very highest levels in the federal government who have cheated on their taxes (two of them actually withdrew when they couldn't stand the ensuing heat)
20. Labeled returning U.S. military veterans as possible terrorists who are "dangerous to the nation"
21. Ordered that the word "Terrorism" no longer be used in exchange for "man-made disasters"

22. Appointed thirty-two czars to top positions in the federal government with **NO** oversight by Congress

23. Spent $200 million to buy three Gulfstream jets to haul Pentagon brass and members of Congress. Is there any reason to believe that these "servants of the people" couldn't fly on United or Delta?

Bibliography

Sources for this book and recommended readings for further study

Beck, Glenn. *Common Sense: The Case Against an Out-of-Control Government.* New York, Simon & Schuster, 2009.

Brookhiser, Richard. *What Would the Founders Do?* New York, Basic Books, 2006.

Buckner, F. Melton, Jr. *The Quotable Founding Fathers: A Treasury of 2,500 Wise and Witty Quotations from the Men and Women Who Created America,* New York, Fall River Press, 2008.

Ellis, Edward S. *The Life of Colonel David Crockett,* Honolulu, Hawaii, University Press of the Pacific, 2004.

Hutson, James H. *The Founders on Religion: A Book of Quotations,* Princeton, NJ, Princeton University Press, 2005.

Levin, Mark R. *Liberty and Tyranny: A Conservative Manifesto.* New York, Simon & Schuster, 2009.

McClanahan, Brion (Ph.D.) *The Politically Incorrect Guide to the Founding Fathers.* Washington, D.C., Regnery Publishing, 2009.

Paine, Thomas. *Common Sense.* New York, Fall River Press, 1995.

Paul, Ron. *The Revolution: A Manifesto.* New York, Grand Central Publishing, 2008.

Shlaes, Amity. *The Forgotten Man: A New History of the Great Depression,* New York, HarperCollins, 2007.

Skousen, W. Cleon. *The Making of America: The Substance and Meaning of the Constitution.* National Center for Constitutional Studies, 1985.

Skousen, W. Cleon. *The 5000 Year Leap: The 28 Great Ideas That Changed the World.* National Center for Constitutional Studies, 1981.

Bibliography

Sources from the Internet

Wikipedia, the Free Encyclopedia, http://en.wikipedia.org/wiki/Main_Page

U.S. National Debt Clock: Real Time, http://usdebtclock.org/

Snopes.com: Rumor Has It, http://www.snopes.com/politics/ballot/athenian.asp

Randall G. Holcombe, "The Growth of the Federal Government in the 1920s," *The Cato Journal*, Volume 16, Number 2, Fall 1996, http://www.cato.org/pubs/journal/cj16n2-2.html

usgovernmentspending.com, http://www.usgovernmentspending.com/us_20th_century_chart.html

govtrack.us: a civic project to track Congress, http://www.govtrack.us/congress/billtext.xpd?bill=hj111-5

New York Congressman Jose E. Serrano Web site, http://serrano.house.gov/

Stephen C. Erickson, *The Entrenching of Incumbency: Reelections in the U.S. House of Representatives, 1790— 1994*, https://www.cato.org/pubs/journal/cj14n3/cj14n3-2.pdf

Archiving Early America, http://www.earlyamerica.com/earlyamerica/freedom/doi/text.html

Archiving Early America, http://www.earlyamerica.com/earlyamerica/freedom/constitution/text.html

USATODAY.com, http://www.usatoday.com/news/politicselections/vote2004/countymap.htm

BUY A SHARE OF THE FUTURE IN YOUR COMMUNITY

These certificates make great holiday, graduation and birthday gifts that can be personalized with the recipient's name. The cost of one S.H.A.R.E. or one square foot is $54.17. The personalized certificate is suitable for framing and will state the number of shares purchased and the amount of each share, as well as the recipient's name. The home that you participate in "building" will last for many years and will continue to grow in value.

Here is a sample SHARE certificate:

YES, I WOULD LIKE TO HELP!

I support the work that Habitat for Humanity does and I want to be part of the excitement! As a donor, I will receive periodic updates on your construction activities but, more importantly, I know my gift will help a family in our community realize the dream of homeownership. **I would like to SHARE in your efforts against substandard housing in my community!** *(Please print below)*

PLEASE SEND ME _____ SHARES at $54.17 EACH = $ $_____

In Honor Of: _____

Occasion: (Circle One)   HOLIDAY   BIRTHDAY   ANNIVERSARY

        OTHER: _____

Address of Recipient: _____

Gift From: _____   *Donor Address:* _____

Donor Email: _____

I AM ENCLOSING A CHECK FOR $ $_____ PAYABLE TO HABITAT FOR HUMANITY OR PLEASE CHARGE MY VISA OR MASTERCARD *(CIRCLE ONE)*

Card Number _____   Expiration Date: _____

Name as it appears on Credit Card _____   Charge Amount $ _____

Signature _____

Billing Address _____

Telephone # Day _____   Eve _____

PLEASE NOTE: Your contribution is tax-deductible to the fullest extent allowed by law.
Habitat for Humanity • P.O. Box 1443 • Newport News, VA 23601 • 757-596-5553
www.HelpHabitatforHumanity.org

LaVergne, TN USA
22 October 2009
161749LV00004B/2/P